Tsumommy!

✦

Riding the Wave of Motherhood

Brenna Barzenick

iUniverse, Inc.
New York Bloomington

Tsumommy!

Riding the Wave of Motherhood

iUniverse books may be ordered through booksellers or by contacting:

iUniverse
1663 Liberty Drive
Bloomington, IN 47403
www.iuniverse.com
1-800-Authors (1-800-288-4677)

ISBN: 978-0-595-49134-6 (pbk)
ISBN: 978-0-595-49667-9 (cloth)
ISBN: 978-0-595-60979-6 (ebk)

Printed in the United States of America

iUniverse rev. date 10/16/2008

*This book is dedicated with love and gratitude
to my husband, children, and all mothers across the universe.*

Contents

Acknowledgments

I must first express gratitude to my wonderful husband, Jay, for his support, encouragement, and love. You are my number one cheerleader. Thank you for appreciating and recognizing the job that I do as a mother. I am the luckiest woman in the world. I love you.

I wish to thank my precious children, Drew and Jay, for being who you are. You both have taught me so much, and even though you are young now, your spirits are so bright and pure. Keep that with you forever, and you will always have peace within. Thank you for choosing me to be your mommy. I love you so much.

Thank you to my mom, Alice, for being such a magnificent example of what a mother should be. You are always there for me. I have learned so much from you (except for ironing and cooking). And thank you for being so richly involved in my children's lives—they adore you.

Thank you to my dad, Philip, for always supporting me and allowing me to believe that great things are in my future. I am blessed to have inherited your sense of humor and playful manner. Perseverance, intense focus, and confidence are your trademarks—thank you for the guidance.

I must also express gratitude to my grandparents, J. D. and Virginia Addison and Louise Monteleone Smith, for simply loving me with all of your hearts. Your influence made me the person I am today. I miss you all, but I know you are smiling down upon me from heaven.

Thank you to my sister, Kristin—you are the most courageous woman I know. Watching you raise your children has helped me to become a better mother. Having a sister to lean on and love is a true blessing. For my brother, Adam—you are amazing. Your brilliance shines in all that you do. You are one of the good guys, for sure.

Thank you, Piper, my sister-in-law, for all of your positive feedback with my writing. I have enjoyed our voyage together into motherhood. Thank you to my in-laws, Walter and Peggy Barzenick, for your support and love and for doing such an excellent job of raising your son.

Elena Keegan, my soul sister, my BFF, I love you. Your light shines on the world. Thank you for guiding me through my fears.

Thank you, Paul Sawyer, for your expert eyes. Your advice and editing skills are superb.

Thank you, Doug Brown, for spending time sharing your story and your experiences. You have been a fantastic resource for me.

Thank you, Joan Davis, my friend and editor at the *Daily Star*. You have nurtured me as a writer. You keep me on track with your professional knowledge and your experiences as a mother and grandmother. Thank you, Lil Mirando, managing editor of the *Daily Star*, for giving me the opportunity to write in your newspaper. Thank you to all of the devoted readers of "Tales from the Crib." I appreciate all of your nice comments and feedback.

For Gwen Gerhardt, Chris McNair, Ann Beegle, Teal Martin, and Dr. Nick Landry for taking time out of your busy lives to read the early drafts of my manuscript.

Thank you, Jimmy and Lillian Maurin, for your encouragement and assistance with my original draft.

Thank you to my son's godparents, Tommy and Vikki Chauvin, for your warm and comfortable friendship, your love, and your laughter. Your marriage and love for each other have been an inspiration to Jay and me from day one.

To my chi sister, Ashley Sandage, the most productive woman I know, thank you for your love and support. I will always treasure our journey together. You are very special to me.

Thank you, Chris and Becky Leumas, for your friendship and love.

Thank you to Michael Conlin, my former business partner, neighbor, and friend for allowing me to be the stay-at-home mommy that I am. And thank you, Shelly Conlin, for your friendship, advice, and reasoning. As a registered nurse and a mom, you have managed to comfort my worries many times.

Thank you, Geri and Bruce O'Krepki, for putting up with my corny jokes and puns during our runs together.

Thank you, Mrs. Linda Link, my high school English teacher, for sharing your love of language with me. I knew I was hooked when you first introduced the word *ubiquitous* on a vocabulary test.

Thank you, Jo Ellen Bezou, my brilliant friend and confidante. My smooth path would have been bumpy if not for you.

For my book club members, Johnny Chauvin, Pat Dunn, Suzanne Durham, Cliff White, and Vikki Chauvin. I am so grateful for our friendship, laughter, and conversation.

Thank you to Mrs. Frances Chauvin and the entire Chauvin family for making me feel like part of your family.

Thank you, Robin Belgard, for taking the time to print all of my drafts.

A huge thanks to the staff at iUniverse: Phil Whitmarsh, Jason Straw, Sarah Disbrow, Jenn Taylor, Shelley Rogers, and all of the brilliant editors and designers who worked on my book. I thank you all for your professionalism, efficiency, and impressive knowledge of the publishing industry. iUniverse is the perfect fit for me.

Thank you, Jennifer Bartels and Nancy Chambless Perilloux, for your artistic vision and wisdom. Special thanks to Marena Monteleone, Dr. Pamela Payment, Marguerite Walter, Cathy Kemp, Carole McAllister, Ashley Ferrand, Marcella Collins, Patricia Westmoreland, Patricia Bender, Michelle Klein, Kirk Hood, Kim Shockley, Dr. Lisa Clark, Marsha Adams, Vicki Nicely, and Robin Chauvin for your encouragement and support.

And for all of the beautiful, smart, and vibrant women in my life—I love you all.

Preface

I consider motherhood as a journey across our planet. My journey has taken me over mountains (of laundry), oceans (of spilled Kool-Aid), and deserts (of dried macaroni). What a wonderful trip it is, but how exhausting! Motherhood has also picked me up and dropped me in front of a computer keyboard, begging me to tell a story.

Years ago, I wrote a medical advice column titled "Joint Effort." The column was published monthly in my hometown newspaper, the *Daily Star*. As a physical therapist, I was comfortable dispensing information about common ailments such as tennis elbow, trigger finger, and low back pain. I have always had a knack for writing, and at the time I was just thrilled to have a forum to share my expertise as a therapist.

After becoming pregnant with my first child, writing became a back-burner project. I could only focus on the miracle growing inside of me, and I knew then to hang up my writing hat. Years passed and two children later, I was approached by Lil Mirando, managing editor of the *Daily Star,* to write a parenting column. At first I declined, knowing that just being a mom certainly didn't qualify me to give parenting advice. Besides, I was always the one that dashed for the parenting section of the bookstore looking for advice.

I knew that one ingredient for successful writing is a clear mind. My mind was fuzzy at best, and that has not changed. Having babies will do that to you. I soon decided to surrender to that fact and just go for it. I contacted Lil and committed to writing a new column that I called "Tales from the Crib." I assured Lil that by no means could I give real advice, but I would be happy to share a few stories about my experiences as a stay-at-home mother. She liked the idea.

With the success of my column, I decided to compile my stories into a book. Thus, *Tsumommy!* was born (and this time it wasn't so painful).

Thank you for your interest in my story. I welcome you in with open arms and a big smile!

Chapter 1

The Devil Wears Pampers

Growing up, I never really liked kids, even though I was one. I didn't like playing dolls or pretending to be a mommy. I did like having an Easy-Bake oven because I could eat cake mix to my heart's content. I managed to play with Barbie dolls, including Ken, but I much preferred G.I. Joe and cowboys. Instead of living it up in her Malibu penthouse, Barbie ended up with a shaved head, riding in one of G.I. Joe's tanks. I imagined her to be a war correspondent with a coordinating flak jacket and helmet.

I guess being raised by a Marine Corps father who was also a Vietnam veteran and a state police officer affected my girly side growing up. Even as I approached the teenage years, I still didn't like kids. I was far too busy applying extra-thick Barbie-esque makeup and hunting for my teenaged Ken to bother with things like babysitting, for instance.

Even in college, I busted my buns waiting tables to earn extra money, all the while avoiding easy babysitting money. I had looked at kids as unfamiliar but curious objects and always from a distance, like a museum exhibit. Up until a few years ago, I thought the children's museum was a place that housed the Amazing Bearded Child or the half monkey, half two-year-old … Hmm, I think that one is living with me now.

The primary focus in my twenties was the ever-important me. It was all about *me*. Me, me, and more of *me*. *Me* could roam free and just *be*. Now *me* is not free and has a new name: Mom-my. Oh, the places you'll go!

Enter my midthirties. The deafening sound of my biological alarm clock was in my ear, and the snooze button did not work any longer. I had a job, a car, a husband, a house, a dog, and I guess I needed one of those too—a baby. I was blessed with a beautiful daughter who was piglet pink and forever cooing. I was told she had a "perfect head" when she was born. What a sigh of relief—now we won't have to join the circus. I still felt out of my league and unsure of my motherly skills. If I would have babysat just once! In the early months, I could have been Lucille Ball in the candy factory, unable to keep up with the assembly line of diapers, spit-up, breastfeeding, and swaddling. (The swaddling thing is still a mystery to me.) So here I am, mother of two, and now, "mother of two" always follows my name.

Motherhood is the most rewarding job on earth. It is the most important job I will ever have. Could someone get me a chalkboard so I can write these lines over and over and convince myself they are true? I will offer a revised edition. Motherhood is as rewarding as earning an Olympic gold medal but is as difficult as climbing Mt. Everest while wearing a blindfold, a thong, and roller skates. It is the most important job I will ever have. Unless I become the next national security advisor. Condi is unflappable, but put her in a room with a couple of two-year-olds, and I'd bet she would be back on Air Force One in no time.

There, I said it. Not the Condoleezza part, the I'm-not-sure-I'm-cut-out-for-full-time-motherhood part. It is hard. It is tiring. It may require medication.

When I was pregnant with my second child, I became possessed by Mary Poppins, umbrella and all. I had visions of carefree romping and unbridled twirling in playgrounds across our land. I would bring the kids to the zoo, the library, and of all places, the children's museum. I would bake gluten-free cookies for them, sew their clothes, and unplug the television. We would listen to classical music, jazz ensembles, and Spanish guitar. We would make crafts, practice yoga, and sing folk songs around the campfire we ignited with a rock and a stick.

How could I be this super mommy while working a real job? Then, the big decision came: sell my business and become, drum roll please … a stay-at-home mom. I took that title literally, because that is mostly what I do, stay at home. Pajamas until noon—that is my life.

I do have to say, since entering a new career as a stay-at-home mom, I have received additional benefits compared to my other career as a health-care provider. For example, I get endless hugs and adoring love from my babies. I mean, what job offers perks like that these days? I imagine the rise in sexual harassment lawsuits has put an end to those workplace moments.

I recently read in a *"Dear Abby"* column that a stay-at-home mother works, on average, ninety-one hours a week. Of course, there is not a salary or a 401(k) involved. Sick leave and vacation days are unheard of. It is all overtime, and if she were to be paid, the projected salary was something like $130,000 a year. Honey, are you listening?

As a stay-at-home mom, I have become a different woman than I ever imagined I would be. My life is paradoxical. I laugh more, but I cry more. I relax more, but I obsess more. I think more, but I forget more. I play more, but I work more. Much more. With each year of being home, my brain cells have died off at an exponential rate. With each cesarean section came a complimentary lobotomy. (See, not all managed-care plans are bad.) Simple addition without a calculator is like a Mensa examination for me. I cannot remember the names of familiar people, and I keep calling the dog Ginger. His name is Sam. I used to know all the answers on *Jeopardy!*. Now I get confused watching *The Price is Right*. The showcases puzzle me for some reason. I also attribute my memory loss and lack of smarts to the constant demands set forth by my children. If my daughter wants something, she will not stop until she eventually breaks me down. I think she could easily be a hostage negotiator when she grows up.

To balance out my stay-at-home duties, my husband and I try to catch a movie once in a while. We really do not care what it is just as long as it is not animated. We like the darkness, the snacks, and the Dolby surround sound. There is one movie I would love to see that is called *The Devil Wears Pampers*. Oops, I mean *Prada*.

My job beckons, as I sit here to write. I hear "Mommy!" in a climbing crescendo coming my way. I must say, with each day, I am learning to love the life I am in. My identity has changed, but I like the new woman in the mirror. Tired but wiser. She has managed to salvage the repressed *me* and has surrendered to the best job of all: motherhood.

Chapter 2

The Prince and the Pee-Pee

Boys will be boys. Whoever coined this phrase knew what they were talking about. In many ways, raising a son is quite different than raising a daughter. Of course, the basics remain the same—nurture, comfort, provide shelter, and give lots of love. But from there, things change.

Boys are wild. I do not mean that in a negative way, only in a programmed-different, caveman-connection sort of way. I noticed these inherent differences very early on. And I mean *very* early. My son had been in this world for about thirty seconds when he peed across the room. My husband, my doctor, and the anesthesiologist all cheered with delight—*Atta boy!*—secretly calculating the amplitude and distance. I realized this is why guys are so good at math and physics. It is because they start analyzing and measuring very early.

So began the male bonding. I do feel very blessed to have a girl and a boy. We do not have to wonder what it would be like to raise the other gender. We have the yin and yang of the species, the Macintosh and the Microsoft, the V8 engine and the diesel engine. Neither is better, just different (except for the V8).

For example, I do not recall my daughter being so interested in balls. As a toddler, she would sit quietly and look at books, carefully examine the delicate petals of a flower, or compose a cutting-edge nursery rhyme. When my son sees a ball, regardless of what he is doing, he barrels toward it, excitedly chanting, "Ba-ba-ba." Look out if there is another male around. Chests will be pounded, and a game of catch will ensue. This could be anywhere. Grocery stores, restaurants, it doesn't matter. Can't you see we are playing ball here! Why is this so? I tried to think of all the spheres and round objects in men's lives. Invention of the wheel, planetary exploration, and world domination, among others.

There is also a peculiar little gesture that *all* men do when they meet my son. The unexplainable, ubiquitous "Give me five." No one has ever asked my little girl to give them five. Why do men do this? Someone tell me, please. If my son is sleepy or shy and doesn't give them five, I feel his baby-manhood is questioned. So I must say, "Oh, he's just tired. He always gives five. Would one or two do for today?"

Language skills are another interesting area to explore. I taught both of my children baby sign language, one of the greatest gifts I have given myself. However, my son chooses to use baby signs instead of trying to talk. His first intelligible word was *donut*. See, all of those educational episodes of *The Simpsons* are paying off. Maybe it is not a boy thing but a second-child thing. My daughter experienced the likes of Mozart in the womb, symphony music in the birthing room, and a set of Brittanicas for her first birthday. Her first word was *totalitarianism*. Just kidding, it was actually *socialist republic*. Actually that was two words, but who's counting?

Odors and sounds are another area for discussion. He still has puppy breath but stinky feet. When he passes gas or burps, he laughs a deep belly laugh. Only on Earth a short while or so, and he knows this is what he is supposed to do. He loves hammers, or anything resembling a hammer, and banging them on all surfaces. "Me must destroy and crush fragile object!" Caveman influence, I imagine.

Boys. You gotta love them. Rough, sweaty, and smelly, but so snuggly and kissable.

Chapter 3

Would You Like Bacteria with That?

For the past ten days or so, my family has hosted an unwelcome guest. It has messed up our beds, sat in our chairs, and has even tasted the porridge. It has affected Baby Bear, Mama Bear, and Sister Bear and seems to be nipping at the heels of Daddy Bear. This is not your neighborhood Goldilocks—this is *rotavirus*, the dreaded stomach flu, and it seems to be living happily ever after in our GI tracts.

Over the course of a week, I have bleached more porcelain than a Hollywood dentist. As a matter of fact, the Clorox corporation sent a note thanking me personally for a recent spike in sales. I have repeatedly washed sheets, comforters, mattress covers, pillow cases, and even the dog, trying to get some control back in my household. Even though I've killed off every virus and bacteria in a five-mile radius, I still feel ostracized by the world. Just mentioning the words *stomach* and *bug* in the same sentence sends people running for cover. It reminds me of the movie trailer for *The Blob*, people panicking, screaming, and running from the hideous ooze coming their way.

The mailman obviously got wind of our plague and has hired a helicopter pilot to airdrop our packages in the front yard. Apparently, he thinks of *us* as the carriers now and wants to stamp out any notion of transmittal. "Tower, this is Maverick, target engaged. Locked in. Three, two, one, fire!" Now picture a little parachute attached to a small box of the latest feminine product sample gliding down ever so gently into my yard. The box did say it had wings. How embarrassing.

Since the entire malaise started, I've been doing my own detective work on rotavirus and trying to figure out how we could have possibly been exposed. I'll call it CSI—colon stomach investigation. I have finally narrowed it down to one suspect: the fast-food restaurant with the indoor play yard, a.k.a. my golden arch enemy.

About fourteen days ago (note the incubation period here), my kids begged me to play in the indoor playground while we were in the drive-thru, picking up a hearty meal of trans fats and chicken parts. After spotting the colorful playground, my daughter said, "Mommy, you never let us go in to eat. We just want to play for fifteen minutes, please, please. And, Mommy, we both have socks on, so you don't have to buy them." I was not ready for the battle and agreed to let them play for a little while.

Normally, I prepare myself for this type of outing. I treat it as an urban survival mission. I will run recon on the place, looking for children with obvious rashes, foamy drool, and super-snotty noses. I also scan the place for the rule-breaker kid who is climbing around on the equipment in cowboy boots. Did the parents not see the "Socks must be worn in the playground at all times" sign? Not that little feet are the problem anyway. I mean, I've never seen a child with toenails that looked like corn chips. Nail fungus does not seem prevalent among the eight-and-under crowd.

That day, the place didn't look all that busy, and I figured, what the heck, I'll be spontaneous for a change. For a brief moment, I felt I was a great mother, doing something wonderful for my children. I was feeding them nuggets, french fries, and Sprite and then letting them play indoors on plastic equipment while the sun was shining brightly outside and fresh air was blowing. What a moment.

So, I gave them the rules before we entered. You must eat first and then play. Yes, ma'am. When I say it is time to go, it is time to go. Yes, ma'am. Do not put your hands near your mouth or eyes when playing. Yes, ma'am. Watch out for the smaller children. Yes, ma'am.

After eating about a third of their food, it was time to hit the playground. We reviewed my rules of engagement along with the rules of the restaurant. Operation McNugget Freedom was off the ground. Wet wipes. Check. Noses wiped. Check. Shoes in cubby hole. Check. Socks on. Check. Watching their excitement and their happy little echoes in the tunnel slide warmed my heart. Shock and awww was the sentiment here.

I observed them playing and finished eating my grilled-chicken salad with fat-free dressing minus the croutons along with the rest of their french fries and chicken nuggets. An Unhappy Meal indeed. I felt like my insides were polymer coated, and I knew I would be leaving feeling battered, stuffed, and preserved.

When it was time to go, the kids did not keep their end of the deal. I had to use phrases such as, "Don't make me climb up there!" and "We will never come here again if you aren't down here in ten seconds!" See, fun for the whole family. I had to resort to the dysfunctional dialogue as a last ditch effort to get them out. You may know the one that goes, "I'm leaving with or without you. I'm getting my purse. Watch me. I'm walking toward the door. I'm almost through the door. I'm touching the handle. You'd better come now …" And so on.

So now we are all recovering nicely from our sickness. The doctor said I could start introducing solid food rather than just clear liquids. Well, guess what my kids asked for. Fast food from the place with the indoor playground. Great. Just great.

Chapter 4

Order in the Carport!

I've always been a list person. I make lists ranging from weekly chores, yearly goals, and home repairs to daily to-dos. With that said, I then have to make a list *of* my lists. My brain automatically sorts, puts things in order, and categorizes them. I think Dewey Decimal was a relative of mine. Yes, I know that is not his real name—Dewey is short for Doolittle or something.

I do have to say this pattern of behavior does have its upside. My trait, for lack of a better diagnosis, came in handy last summer when my sister and I had a garage sale. It was like an Olympic event for obsessive-compulsive people. I trained, I visualized, I conquered! The place looked like Baby Gap, and I know the people who came appreciated the sizing categories, color-coded pricing labels, and the bar-code scanner at the register. I mean, who wouldn't? Toys were sanitized and labeled for age and sex. I also attached a laminated sheet from *Consumer Reports* discussing the learning benefits of each toy and a guarantee of lead-free materials used in their manufacturing. I could tell this was a big hit with my customers—I mean, they whispered, pointed, and glanced back at me. I know they were saying, "Wow, what a great garage sale, and that young woman over there took special care to ensure my child's safety." For an objective pat on the back, I set up an online survey that my customers could visit after they left the garage sale. It only took a minute, and they could win the book, *You Too Can Be This Organized.*

I did review the survey results and came to realize that "crazy lady" and "she ain't got nothin' better to do" are actually compliments.

So, for all of my efforts, I ended up with a financial loss based on the profit-and-loss statement from the garage sale. I am certain this will give me a nice tax break.

Well, I have moved on to another organizing extravaganza. I have begun the task of transitioning my son's room from baby to little boy. This is where I shine. I love every minute of sorting, containerizing, and labeling things. For Valentine's Day, did I want roses, perfume, or chocolate? No, I wanted a self-printing label maker with specialty fonts. And if I craved chocolate, I could make my own little Hershey's Kiss banner with my nifty label machine. I am very easy to please. My husband is a lucky man indeed. Instead of dropping flower petals leading to a bubble bath surrounded by candles, my husband can leave pages from the Container Store catalog. Really, any Office Depot or Shelving Direct catalog will do just fine.

Normally, I can throw out just about anything. Pack rats fear me. They have even hired an assassin to eliminate me, but they just can't seem to dispose of my body. I can throw out Aunt Willie's prized ceramic rooster as easily as I can a broken Lego. An old love letter from the Civil War? Gone, dust mites and all. I can even say bye, bye, bye to most of my children's things. Thank you, Justin Timberlake. Baby bibs, gone. Rocking horse, gone. Monogrammed bath set, gone. Dropping a trailer load off at Goodwill: priceless.

I have reached a tremendous obstacle, however. I consider it a chink in my armor, a Moby Dick to my minnow, a Stridex pad to my pimples. You see, the problem is I cannot get rid of the crib. I've stared at it, pondered over it, and realized that I am not ready to let it go. You would think I could, being that both of my children have never actually slept in it for longer than an afternoon nap. They seem to prefer the warm, cozy space between my husband and me. All the endearing baby pictures of my little ones sleeping soundly in the crib were staged, I'll admit. Well, I guess it can be passed down to my grandchildren one day. Though by then, technology will probably have produced a hover crib or a simulated womb pod for babies.

I recently read that if something is useful or beautiful then keep it; otherwise, throw it away or give it away. Well, the crib is no longer useful, but it is beautiful. Beautiful because it represents motherhood and the tremendous blessing of being given my children. Yes, that is beautiful. I think I'll keep it.

Chapter 5

Musical Beds

I got this big idea several months ago to plan a trip for our anniversary. At first, I felt excitement thinking about just me and my husband on a tropical island without the kids. I envisioned a scene similar to the Corona beer commercial—clear water, tanned feet, and a soothing breeze. Forget the beer, just give me solitude. I was really into my daydream when I was thrust back to reality by a crying baby who needed a boo-boo kissed.

Babies need their mommies, and I was torn about leaving them—something I had never done for more than twenty-four hours. My husband is a sap about leaving our kids, too. We love being a family and sacrifice a lot of "married" time together because of this. Even our nights are not our own; our children always end up in our bedroom by morning.

Of course, they are irresistibly warm and fuzzy, but it is hard to get used to sleeping in one square foot of space. A magician's assistant in a box has more room to move around than we do. Meanwhile, the kids have claim to the entire middle two-thirds of our mattress. Not to mention, my dangling leg is a prime target for the monster under the bed. Some mornings we wake up looking like a litter of puppies—tails here, paws there, bellies on bellies.

During the night, my son likes to burrow into the space between my armpit and chest like a tick. I have tried all kinds of things, including insect repellant with DEET, but he keeps coming back, night after night. My daughter, on the other hand, and I mean literally sleeping *on my other hand*, has started to talk in her sleep. It goes to show that kids really do live in the present, and they do not worry about tomorrow or yesterday. She will mumble things such as, "That's mine," "Watch my cartwheel, Mommy," and "Can we skip washing my hair tonight?" When I talk in my sleep, I'll say things like, "Is the iron off?" "Love your shoes," "What did I just say!" and "Gotta make the donuts."

Since having kids, there is an interesting phenomenon that has arisen in our household. Seasoned parents warned me about it. It's a game I like to call "musical beds." Yes, imagine everyone going to sleep in one place and waking up in a totally different place. If aliens were studying this behavior, they would be puzzled. Even their higher intelligence would not be able to figure out why the big humans let the little humans sleep in their nest, then the big humans move to one of the little human's nests, and then they all switch before sunrise. I don't think we will be abducted by the mother ship anytime soon.

Musical beds has put a new perspective on men getting in touch with their feminine side. One morning, I sleepily stumbled into my daughter's room only to find my handsome, strapping husband sleeping soundly amongst pastel princess sheets while clutching a white, stuffed Build-A-Bear with a rhinestone visor. I'm thinking Spider-Man sheets are in my near future for sure.

My motivation for leaving on a vacation without the kids was really based on sleep, not romance. I realized I would have to leave the country in order to get uninterrupted sleep.

Warning: If you are considering having children, the following statements may be disturbing and may cause a delay in procreating.

For the past four-and-a-half years—yes, years—I have not slept for more than five hours straight without being awakened by one of the children. My kids are terrible sleepers, and one of them always manages to wake up between the hours of 2:00 and 4:00 a.m. Their little internal clocks are set to awaken during a time I refer to as the "witching hours."

One would think I gave birth to two lemurs—they only come out at night and tend to hang and climb on larger objects. I can hear the faint sound of the *Mutual of Omaha's Wild Kingdom* narrator saying, "Quiet, we are observing the behavior of nature's most elusive nocturnal creature, the soft-haired lemur. They are playful, gentle animals but can be territorial among other lemurs of the same age. They sometimes defy the matriarchal leader of the pack, who has to discipline them by taking away their eucalyptus." Candy equals eucalyptus where I come from.

After traveling by land, by air, and by sea, we finally arrived at our Caribbean bungalow. The kids are safe at home with my mom, and I'm starting to loosen up a bit. The turquoise water is calling me but the bed speaks louder. I want to sleep like a teenager again. I want to sleep like I'm under general anesthesia. But do I? No, I am preset to wake up at 2:00 a.m., dreaming of being next to my little puppies. This is going to be a long vacation.

Chapter 6

Sunscream

In early spring, we took a short trip to Florida with the kids. Every time I pack for a trip, I am amazed at all of the things a mother must think to bring. Clothing that ranges for varying temperatures like forty-degree nights to seventy-degree days, pajamas, slippers, non-skid socks for the baby, swim diapers, regular diapers, and overnight diapers. Safety outlet plugs, Clorox wipes for the bathroom, pillows, sterile bedspreads, and balcony nets. The list goes on to include flip-flops, water shoes, nice going-out-to-dinner shoes, and all of Mommy's shoes. Dad is only allowed to bring one pair because of the space constraints in our Suburban that seats about fifty.

Tangent alert—speaking of Chevy Suburbans, I feel like I need a commercial driver's license, a CB radio, and a 1-800-How's-My-Driving? number posted on the bumper every time I drive the thing. I wait to hear the beep-beep-beep sound when I put it in reverse, you know, like a backhoe. Fighter pilots who land on aircraft carriers have reported difficulty parallel parking the Suburban, so don't honk at me on Main Street.

There are advantages to driving the love child of the C-130 aircraft and a city bus. First, everyone knows you are a mom on the way to carpool. No need for the Baby on Board sign in the rear window; just get out of my way. I have precious cargo on board, and they are late for gymnastics! Sometimes, when driving the monster on the highway, I wish I had missile launchers on the steering wheel for those left-lane drivers on the interstate. Sorry for the SUV rant; kids tend to get me off track a lot. Lots. Of. Frag. Mented. Thoughts.

OK, we're back. Other things necessary for trips include medicine for every ailment or illness that could possibly affect your child. One would think I was going to Zimbabwe with the kids when, in reality, there is a pharmacy on every corner. Believe it or not, there are doctors practicing in Florida. I have to bring cough medicine. Not just one bottle of regular cough medicine, I have to pack an assortment for each child. The one for daytime revs up my daughter but knocks the baby out for hours. His nighttime medicine keeps her awake and so on and so on. I have to bring Motrin and Tylenol in case of a bad fever, yellow Triaminic, Benadryl for the possibility of a jellyfish or Portuguese man-o-war sting (or a quiet night with the hubby), swimmer's-ear drops, pink-eye drops, and rattlesnake antivenom (oh, wait, that is for the Arizona vacation).

Then there is the subject of sunscreen. This was going to take up about four long paragraphs, but I decided to keep it short instead of writing a sequel to *War and Peace*. Although, sometimes our car trips could be summarized by that very title … Well, I am always on a quest for the best sunscreen. The contents of my cabinet, in spite of the labeled shelves ranking each bottle of sunscreen according to SPF, rivals the earth's ozone layer for UV protection. My children are a dermatologist's dream. They will thank me for their pasty white bodies when they turn forty. When I was a kid, I burned and blistered. Then my mother put a white T-shirt over my swimsuit for a few days. I couldn't wait for the skin to peel. I had fun peeling the layers off and trying to see how big of a piece I could get. It was almost like a medal from battle. The bigger the sheet of skin, the better my tan would be underneath.

Aside from Kraft Easy Mac, I do have to say the best invention ever is the built-in DVD player in the car. No more creative alphabet games or silly, educational songs. Now just hit play, and let the movie do all the work. When it is over, I do have to fumble feverishly to put a new movie in before the crying starts. I feel like I have twenty seconds to defuse a bomb before all hell breaks loose. I have the National Highway Traffic Safety Association Web site as my home Web page, but I will still unbuckle at seventy-five miles per hour and sacrifice life and limb so the little demanders can be happy. I have gotten very good at driving with one toe while reaching back to put a movie in. I knew all that yoga would come in handy.

I won't even go into what my daughter has to bring in the way of purses, stuffed animals, writing utensils, lip gloss, movie selections, books, bags for shells, pink polka-dotted umbrellas, and Hello Kitty sunglasses. Boys are a bit easier in this department—he only needs a diaper and a sippy cup for the road.

Once we arrive at the beach, my husband must get two luggage carts for our three-day weekend. With his math brain, he calculated that each child plus their mommy requires forty-two cubic feet of space for traveling. It has taken me one week to pack for three days and will probably take another week to unpack. All I know is I am prepared for any disaster, illness, or ultraviolet radiation that may come my way.

Chapter 7

Save the Newspaper

My son has officially entered full-fledged toddlerdom. He is in a state of constant motion and proves that Sir Isaac Newton's Laws of Motion are indeed alive and well. I'll bet Sir Newton had a little one who was actually in the apple tree throwing things down on his head. Just like my children inspire me, I'm sure his did too. My son defies gravity, teeters on wobbly chairs to reach untouchables, and leaps from furniture with a single bound—he is Super Baby! And green beans are his kryptonite. I do feel he is a cross between Evel Knievel and Swee'Pea from Popeye.

In addition to his physical accomplishments, he has also developed a healthy temper. There must be a switch or countdown timer in the brain that goes off around the age of two that says, "Scream. Whatever you do, just scream. This, and this alone, will get the old lady to give you whatever you want." The switch must also be connected to a network of varying screams designed for greater challenges like staying in the car seat or fingernail trimming. I am currently working on a patent for the domestic version of the limousine privacy shield for my car. I can see the infomercial now … kids screaming and begging, Mom pushes the big green button, the screen goes up between the front and backseats, Mom smiles while the kids' lips are still moving and their uvulas are strumming—and there is silence. Call now and the first ten people will get the handy Low-Voltage Kids' Tazer for just $9.95.

As far as clipping his fingernails, one would think I was trying to put horseshoes on him. He squirms, screams, stiffens, and goes floppy. He also goes into a maneuver similar to an alligator death roll. I have decided that the trauma induced from pinning him down is too much for the both of us. Plus, the screaming has alarmed the neighbors. With all the practice I get trying to trim nails and change diapers, I could do really well in the calf-roping division at the local rodeo. Lately, I've been keeping the nail clippers in the car, and when he falls asleep, I clip. This is an exciting moment in motherhood, trimming a sleeping baby's nails. I need to get out more!

My daughter never falls asleep in the car, so I have to use the "you will get worms under them" line in order to trim her nails. This works as well as the lice comment when she won't wash her hair. As I've said before, I have started a psychotherapy trust fund for my kids. The good part is she may become an entomologist with her frequent lice and worm encounters.

My son has also reached the naked milestone. He loves to run around with nothing on and pee everywhere. I feel like we have a new puppy in the house. He pees on the carpet, whines at night, and bites. My next step is putting down newspaper to train him.

Next to the "scream" switch in the toddler brain is the "play with your food" switch. Invariably, I can walk across the kitchen floor barefooted and every food group, the entire FDA pyramid, will be stuck on my feet. He throws food and mixes gross things together. What is on the menu tonight? Peas smashed in strawberry yogurt, chocolate milk poured on meatloaf, and Play-Doh blended into mashed potatoes. He likes to put his food in a glass of water and wash it like a raccoon. And, I have crowned him the King of Backwash. I will grab my refreshing bottle of water and take a big swig, only to discover food particles floating around. Disgusting! If I'm really thirsty, I'll wait for the particles to settle and drink it anyway. (I have also been known to eat food off of his shirt, his lap, and, I'll admit, even the floor if it is a worthy morsel. Part of motherhood, I guess.)

My body has adapted to motherhood via the animal kingdom. My feet have evolved into mother gorilla feet. I can pick up just about anything off the floor with my feet. It is convenient and promotes hamstring flexibility. If this were an Olympic event, I would surely win gold. At least I could join the circus. "Come one, come all! See the monkey-footed mother! She is hideous but gets so much done!"

Another part of being two years old is repetition. Repetition. He listens to the same song over and over and over. It is a children's song, but if you play it backward, a sinister voice says, "Send Mother to crazy house. Send Mother to crazy house!" The U.S. military could use the song for prisoner interrogation. Believe me, the prisoner would rat out Bin Laden's location in a heartbeat if they had to hear The Wiggles' "Hot Potato" song two hundred times in a row. "OK, OK, he's in the fourth bunker to the right, just over the hill. If you come to a daisy patch, you've gone too far." A national security problem solved.

So, to summarize, if you come to my house any time soon, expect to see a naked baby and a wigged-out mother with odd-looking feet. And remember … don't drink the water!

Chapter 8

Easter Basket(case)

Well, the Easter Bunny visited our house this year and brought gobs of candy to my children. I thought rabbits were herbivores, vegetable proponents, so how did he become a candy peddler? It seems as though all holidays are turning into candy festivals. Halloween, Valentine's Day, and Easter all center around refined sugar. Pretty soon, obscure holidays that are listed on my Day Planner calendar will be another excuse to buy mounds of candy for the children. I'm sure I'll hear that Arbor Day will be cause for celebration, and we must buy miniature chocolate trees to celebrate. I think the sugar industry has a lobbyist with lots of PAC money visiting the old Easter Bunny these days.

To ensure that she was the recipient of a candy cornucopia, my thoughtful daughter left an Easter basket on the fireplace hearth with a beautiful picture she colored for the Bunny. She also asked if she should leave a few dollars in the basket, a little money on the side for a few extra Gold Brick eggs. I told her that the Bunny does not spend money because he is a rabbit.

She asked, "Then how does he buy the candy, Mommy?"

"Well, honey, he makes the candy at a factory," I replied.

"Is it in the North Pole near Santa's toy factory?" she countered.

I stammered. OK, think, woman. Where does the Bunny live?

"He has a huge rabbit hole underground in the middle of North America, and this is where the factory is located," I offered.

"Does he know Willy Wonka?" she asked.

"Yes, probably."

"Oh look, Mommy, he must know him because the candy says it right here—*Wonka,*" she pointed out.

I told her, "Oh yeah, that's right, I did read that Willie Wonka is somewhat of a consultant to the Bunny and most likely has stock in the underground hole. He struck a deal with the Bunny to allow his trademarked name to be used on the Bunny's candy."

Blank stares but no more probing questions until she asked, "Does he come down the chimney?"

"No, Santa does that," I said.

"Then how does he get in?" she asked.

(Whew, this is too much thinking on a Sunday morning.)

"He comes in, excuse me, hops in, through the front door," I replied nervously.

"Does he have a key?" she asked.

"No, but we will leave it unlocked for him, honey."

"But that's not *safe*, Mommy," she insisted.

"You are right, honey. I'll send him an e-mail telling him where the key is and the alarm code."

"So he can *read*, Mommy?"

"Uh, yes?" I said, hesitating.

"But I didn't know rabbits could read. Can he talk?" she asked.

"Yes."

"Can he speak Spanish?"

"Sí."

"French?"

"Oui."

"Can he hop on one foot like this?" she asked.

"Yep," I conceded.

"Can he do a cartwheel, Mommy?"

Exhausted, I replied, "I don't know, but I'll re-fur that question to your daddy."

After I'd gotten past this hairy situation, she continued to ask more and more questions regarding the Rabbit.

"Mommy, do you think he watches *American Idol*?"

"No. But he is a big fan of *The Sopranos*," I added. "You see, dear, he has been intrigued with organized crime since the disappearance of Jimmy Hoppa."

Thankfully, the interrogation ended there.

In regards to candy consumption, I do admit that I have made mistakes with my first child. Not one grain of sugar passed through her lips in the first year of her life. When she turned one, I even made a whole-wheat birthday cake for her with applesauce filling and real fruit icing. The soy ice cream was also a nice touch. I wasn't aware the cake would harden overnight into a solid mass resembling mortar mix. Being a physical therapist, I should have known that a one-year-old does not have the arm strength to bust through a cake made of Kevlar and wheat germ. It was truly a scene at the birthday party, with family and friends laughing uncontrollably at me and my cake. Lesson learned. When my son turned one, I bought him the whitest, fluffiest, icing-laden cake I could find, and he easily penetrated it with one swipe. I am such a good mommy!

Because of the sucrose deprivation in the first two years of her life, my daughter has turned into a sugar addict. All she wants to eat is sugar. She even asks to put sugar packets in the Sprite at restaurants. I have been actively searching for a CDU for children under six, you know, a candy dependency unit. We are currently planning an intervention, but we will wait until school is out in case things get ugly.

My neighbor, a mom with three kids, once told me that I should let my kids have sugar because it will actually have the opposite effect than one would expect. She says if children know they can have sugar when they want it, then they won't want it all of the time. We do have a running joke that her house is the Gingerbread House, and my daughter is now nicknamed Gretel. The shutters on her house are deceivingly woodlike, but up close, you will see they are actually graham crackers. The Pez dispenser is cleverly disguised as a mailbox, and the ceiling fans are actually cotton-candy spinners. She must be right because this principle seems to be working on my son. He loves sugar but will also choose broccoli over M&M'S.

So, this Easter, I will sit back and watch the kids rabidly consume the contents of their baskets. I will put up with hyperactivity, mood swings, and chocolate mustaches. I am actually referring to myself after picking through the baskets to find the peanut butter eggs. One for the kids, ten for me … don't you just love the holidays!

Chapter 9

Lost in Translation

Years ago, when I was deciding on what I was going to be when I grew up, I thought of many exciting and rewarding careers. My first choice was to be an aerospace engineer. The truth is that I didn't know what an aerospace engineer actually did (not that I do now), but it sounded impressive and goal driven. The physics, the graphs, and the whole NASA thing started to bore me, so I decided at the ripe old age of eight to be a nun. Well, that lasted about a week, when I was told that I would not be able to wear shorts, I had to wear white after Labor Day, and I would forever be in SAS comfort shoes. Even at eight years old, I knew a stylish shoe when I saw one, and Sister Mary Esther did not own a pair. So, a hundred semesters later and well into my twenties, I finally became a physical therapist. I now realize that being a speech therapist would have better served me, because I may have had a chance of understanding my two-year-old when he talks.

Being his mother, I can understand survival words such as eat, ball, dog, go, potty, stop, no, Coke, and night-night. But when it comes to full sentences spoken with conviction, I lose him after the first syllable. After a frustrating exchange of guess the words, I call in the expert, my daughter. She brilliantly interprets baby-speak and could make a career of it. Call her the Toddler Whisperer. She can cut through "ba-ba, woo-woo, la" very quickly to tell me, "He wants the light on." Wow! How does she do it? I sometimes wish she could just stay alongside him like the sign-language lady that interprets the president's speech for the hearing impaired.

"I nee gape ike puber land," he proudly states.

Toddler Whisperer translation: "Mom, he said he needs a cape like Superman."

"Oh, yes, got it. Thanks, honey," I tell her.

"I won tun soup and hair pot moved," he will say.

"You want wonton soup and a what?" I ask, puzzled.

She deciphers it again, with eyes rolling. "Nooo, Mom, he wants you to turn on the Harry Potter movie." Again, I am in awe. He has actually learned to retrieve his sister from her room when his requests require compound sentences and conjugated verbs.

Aside from his budding oration skills, he has developed a sense of fashion. He will only wear the shirts that I do not like and refuses for one minute to put on my favorite ones that look great with his gorgeous blue eyes. I've tried to outsmart him by saying the ugly shirt was dirty, but it doesn't work—he will demand to wear it anyway. Then there are the tags. I've cut off more tags than a shoplifter on Christmas Eve. Wise women say that you are supposed to allow children to express their individuality in order for them to develop self-esteem. But, come on, there are times when I just have to put my foot down. Like the time he wanted to wear my daughter's pink Disney shirt with a mermaid on it to the annual tractor-pull celebration. I mean, we all know that event screams camouflage, overalls, and shrimp boots.

Yes, my former drooling little bundle of giggles is now becoming a little man. He is an individual who expresses his likes and dislikes with vigor and wants to do everything for himself. He will let me know quickly that anything green does not qualify as food, unless it is a Popsicle or a gummy vitamin. He wants to brush his own teeth, and when he finally relents to me, he limits my intrusion to the two front teeth only. When I try to get back to the molars, he clinches down with pit bull–like force. Periodontal disease, here we come.

As independent as he is, I am comforted to know that my son still wants his mommy close by for a quick hug and a kiss, a spin around the room, or an airplane ride on my feet. And, I know for sure what he's saying when I hear, "Me lub you, Mommy."

Chapter 10

Food for Thought

On Mother's Day, we made a regular appearance at my mom's house for lunch. She cooks for just about every holiday and continues to spoil my husband with gourmet meals. Some men wince at the idea that their wife will one day look like their mother-in-law, but my husband only smiles, picturing me in an apron standing at the stove, actually cooking. I have a confession to make—I despise cooking. I certainly did not inherit the kitchen gene from my mom, who in the previous sentence would have said, "I have a *confection* to make." She can whip up a fabulous meal, even with minimal ingredients available. I'm not kidding. She is the MacGyver of food preparation. Just give her some yellow mustard, breadcrumbs, and a ham hock, and bada bing—lunch is served. I, on the other hand, keep buying stuff, hoping that one evening it will get cooked. I am the antithesis of Julia Child. But I do have a very organized pantry; soup labels are in alphabetical order, dry goods are vertically aligned according to height and fiber content, flour sits in Ziploc bags, teasing the weevils who can't get in, and I also have a tiny space allotted for candy. Yes, candy. The freezer has meat stacked in descending order of freshness, and the fish are lined up like they were still swimming in their schools. Everything is labeled with masking tape and a permanent marker in the neatest draftsman font, indicating the freshness date. My brain replays the "starving children in Africa" tape every time I have to purge the freezer. Wanna see starving children? Come to my house around dinnertime every evening.

Around 3:00, I start thinking about dinner. What restaurant can we go to tonight? No, really, it does cross my mind to prepare a meal for my family. However, I get distracted. *Oprah* is on, and the topic is, what else, starving children in Africa. Therein starts my procrastination. I go to Oprah.com and donate money to the fund for starving children. Motivated that I just clicked my way to a hot meal for the famine stricken, I browse a few more important Web sites that can make a difference in the world. Zappos.com for shoes, Lands End Kids, and, of course, local Doppler radar. I am obsessed with the radar for some reason, and it must be because I'm getting older. I think it goes along with my recent interest in reading the newspaper obituaries and police news. I think my identity has been switched with a senior citizen's, and boy, are they having fun.

All right, it is now 4:00, and I have one hour until the angry mob barges in with forks in hand. Let me browse through a cookbook or two. Chop? I don't think so, takes too long. Peel and wash? Nope, that would be two steps; don't have time for that. Peeling ought to do just fine. Add marjoram? Are you kidding? What I need is thyme. This is too complicated, and Domino's pizza is starting to sound good. I can use the opportunity to teach the baby about triangles based on the pizza slices. Good idea.

On occasion, I do crack down and plan a healthy meal for my kids. This usually occurs after a week's worth of fast food and eating out. I start feeling like we need some organic food to cleanse our bodies, so I prepare this great meal that has taken hours in the kitchen and many dollars from my wallet. I set the table; get everyone's favorite plate, cup, and serving utensils; and call everyone in to eat. Once served, the kids won't eat it. The leafy green vegetables frightened them. You see, they have grown accustomed to chicken nuggets and Easy Mac, which I keep well stocked, like toilet paper. They do not seem to recognize the original shapes of real vegetables and chicken.

Breakfast is an area where I excel. I have perfected the one-hand push on the toaster for the Eggo waffle and can pour milk on cereal with the best of them. The kids love pancakes, and I can actually make a semiedible version of them, provided we have lots of syrup on hand to drown out the taste of my flour Frisbees. The box did say the batter would be lumpy. After my kids eat pancakes for breakfast, they smell like syrup for the rest of the day. It is like the smell has been burned into their hair and lips. This is puzzling, and perhaps I should ask Betty or Duncan why this is so. I bet Aunt Jemima would know.

Well, look at the time. I need to start thinking about dinner. I pledge to do better in the kitchen, and I think I will start by attending a Procrastinator's Anonymous meeting. I think a group is starting in our area sometime in the near future.

Chapter 11

Drag Queen

Last weekend, I decided it would be nice to plan an outing for my husband, Jay, for Father's Day. I would take him to dinner and then to a movie—this would be at least four hours of uninterrupted time with him. I arranged for a babysitter, made dinner reservations, and checked the newspaper for the movie listings. I made sure the kids were bathed, diapered, and smelling nice for the sitter. I also figured she would be capable of microwaving a nutritious meal for them. As I set a couple of Kid Cuisine frozen dinners on the counter, for a moment, I felt like Marie Antoinette. I would be out feasting on a gourmet meal, and my kids would be stuck at home eating processed foods.

I gave the babysitter every phone number available in case of an emergency. She had a long list of numbers, including my cell phone, my husband's cell phone, the restaurant, my mom, my neighbor, our pediatrician, the hospital, and Homeland Security.

We arrived on time for our dinner reservation at precisely 5:30 p.m. I have started to notice that we are eating earlier and earlier. We now have almost a two-hour head start on most people who are heading out on a Saturday night. Retired folks even think we are lightweights. I know we will be assured a table, and our food will be out in plenty of time to get to the movie for 7:00 p.m. Since kids came along, seven o'clock has become the old nine o'clock, and ten o'clock is midnight to us. Obscenely late would be 10:30.

I had sworn off the wonderful baked bread and butter on our table, leaving my mouth free and clear to chat with my husband. We talked mostly about the kids and the cute things they say or do. For some reason, our children seem brighter, funnier, and more loveable than most kids when they are not with us. Attempts were made at discussing world issues, the Iowa caucuses, and even Britney Spears's latest behavior. But after a few minutes, our children made their way back into our conversation.

I was talking about the war in Afghanistan, which lead me to the word *afghan*, which reminded me of blankets, which made me think of snuggling with the kids. Discussion of interest rates made me think of percentages, which brought me to something I read about the percentage of children who suck their thumbs, and I was quickly back to our little ones again. I am hopeless, and Jay is not much better. He redirected our conversation back to interest rates and Alan Greenspan's retirement. But Alan made him think of our son's middle name, and Greenspan made him think of our lawn and throwing balls with the kids.

We finished our meal early, so we had about an hour before the movie started. I also managed to eat half of the bread that I had previously rejected. It kept calling my name, and I do not like to disappoint. Well, so much for the trip to Baskin Robbins.

With plenty of time to spare, we decided to do something a little risky, wild, and totally out of our element. Drag racing. OK, not exactly, but we did ride around our town like a couple of teenagers. We turned up the radio as loud as possible and set the bass on full tilt. I know we fooled a lot of people into thinking we were hip youngsters (as long as they didn't notice our kids' car seats). The sound of my Josh Groban CD blaring from the windows gave us the street cred we longed for. We had looked for an Eminem album, but the only place we could find M&M'S was lodged in the backseat upholstery.

We drove by the college, the mall, and the car wash. We also wanted to see the insurance building that a car drove through last week—our brush with danger. Lots of excitement, eh?

At the red light, I secretly wished for a short race with the guy next to us in the Camaro. If I were driving, it would have happened. There is something to be said about being at a red light in a small town. I have noticed that when I see someone I know, and it looks like we will be side by side at the light, I do my best to accelerate at great speeds to avoid this situation. "Hang on, kids, there's Suzy!" With wheels screeching around the corner, I will run through yellow lights, blast through four-way stops, or drive ten miles per hour so I won't have to give the obligatory wave or acknowledgment. Pretending to be on my cell phone, fumbling with the radio, or turning on a side street are also effective measures of avoidance.

This also happens when I see people I know at the grocery store. First, there is small talk at the produce section. Wow, nice melons. Then, I see them again in the soup aisle for more chatter on the weather and such. Hot out there, huh? By aisle three, I turn the basket around and head to the aisle with less-popular items such as hemorrhoid cream. Certainly people will not want to talk to me there. But, they do.

After roaming the streets for a good half hour, we talked ourselves out of going to the movie. It would not have been fair to the babysitter if we arrived home two hours before she expected, so we went to Walgreens. Yes, Walgreens. What a romantic evening we spent perusing the aisles, looking at greeting cards, body wash, and Band-Aids. This night, to buy more time away from home, we were actually looking for people to talk to in the aisles.

After a simultaneous yawn, we decided it was time to go home. The toy aisle did us in. We were anxious to bring home the little treats we picked up for the kids. As we pulled into the driveway, we could see the children through the window, waving to us excitedly. My husband looked over at me and gently squeezed my hand. His tender gesture said it all—home is where we really want to be.

Chapter 12

The Amazing Spider-Man

I have always loved movies. As a matter of fact, movie going was one of my favorite things to do prior to my darling children entering the world. I am really a movie critic at heart, and back then my goal was to see all of the Academy Award nominees for Best Picture. Now, Meryl Streep, Sidney Poitier, and Al Pacino have all been replaced by Shrek, Spider-Man, and Harry Potter. On top of having to watch animated or children's movies exclusively, I am also subjected to taming the wiggles out of my little boy at the theater. He is good for about thirty minutes of sitting, and then he is ready to get up and move around. These days, the previews alone last thirty minutes, and this certainly cuts into his attention span. At the beginning of the show, I explain to my son that we must use our "inside voices" during the movie. In our house, the "inside voice" does not really qualify as quiet, mine included. Maybe I could change the phrase to "sleeping voice."

Well, the first ten minutes at least usually goes well. He is quiet, calm, and munching on fourteen-dollar popcorn. He leans over to me and says, "Me quiet, Mommy." His little wet whisper in my ear is very cute and feels like a kitten's sneeze. You don't mind it because it is coming from such a sweet little critter. Then, he gets progressively louder, like the commercials on television. "Mommy! Gotta pee-peeee" resonates well in a confined space and always summons a turn-around glare from the person seated in front of us. I then realize I should have named him Dolby, being that he is able to transmit his voice in multidimensional decibels throughout the theater.

It goes without saying that the film industry has a marketing campaign designed to bombard our children with paraphernalia for every movie coming out this summer. It is not enough that our savings account is depleted every time we go to the movies. I wonder if the government could introduce an MSA plan—a movie savings account with tax-free interest. Right now, you simply cannot turn around in any store without seeing Shrek and Spider-Man everywhere. I have bought cereal, crackers, yogurt, and pancakes with movie-character shapes and colors. We also have beach towels, blankets, sheets, and shoes with the same scenes. I'm waiting for a few baby items such as the new Harry Potty-chair, Spider-Man feminine products with cotton webbing for better absorbency, and I even have an idea for a cash-advance business that could advertise Shrek-cashing with no movie credit check!

Well, the movie industry is winning. I recently broke down and bought my son a Spider-Man costume. I considered it a strategy to save money on buying everything else in the world with the character on it. My plan has backfired. You see, my son now thinks he *is* Spider-Man, the amazing Spider-Man, web-weaver extraordinaire. He climbs, jumps, and has even rescued Barbie a few times from harrowing situations. Ken got jealous (but only because Spider-Man didn't rescue him, wink, wink). He throws his web at unsuspecting strangers, but with his still-developing motor-skill coordination, the web-throwing gesture looks semiprofane. The little old lady in the grocery store did not find it amusing and looked befuddled when I said, "Oh, he is throwing his web and needs practice!" I'm sure she wondered, "*What* is this world coming to?" I've even caught him climbing to the top of my pantry shelves, and when I tried to take him down, he told me, "Get my mask, Mommy, and the camera!" Oh boy.

Now, he has completely morphed into Spider-Man and refuses to take off the costume. He sleeps in it, eats in it, and wears it all day, regardless of the food stains and dirt. I wish Spider-Man were a *grime* fighter, because then I would have no complaints. I finally gave up on having him change into real clothes before we go to town. It just wasn't worth the fight. Everyone knows you cannot win against a superhero. News reports cite that Spider-Man has been seen at the local Subway, Guy's grocery store, the Feed and Seed store and the movie theater, of course. I'm sure church is next. God loves all creatures, even arachnids, right?

At present, the costume remains tattered and torn from doing battle with his archenemy, his sister. This does not stop him; it only makes him stronger. He corrects me when I call him "son" or "baby" or "sweetie." "Me not baby, me Spider-Man!" I guess that makes me Spider-Mommy. I knew I shouldn't have gone swimming in the nuclear-waste pond when I was pregnant! And I shouldn't have vacuumed up the rubble from the meteorite that crashed into my living room. That darn cosmic radiation gets me every time!

Chapter 13

Beach Nut

Summer is here, and the pressure is off to get my daughter to school on time. For a few months, I won't have to run out of the house with my hair in a baseball cap and wearing the shirt I slept in. The baby can have his milk in his highchair instead of drinking it while enduring g-force acceleration and fishtails on the way to school. We can stay in our pajamas all day, delay tooth brushing until noon, at least, and eat ice cream for breakfast.

Summer also means frequent trips to the beaches of Florida. This past week, I had a great opportunity to observe my children at the beach. Watching them play brought back a flood of fond memories from my childhood trips to Florida. The beach was always, and still is, my favorite vacation. The warmth of the sun, the smell of the ocean, and the lazy days can be addicting. My memories revolve around trips to Panama City Beach with my grandparents, J. D. and Virginia Addison. We would stay at the Desert Palms Motel owned by their friends, the Coopers. I smile deep inside every time I think about those days.

Back in my single-digit days, the car trip over to the Sunshine State was long but relaxing and educational to boot. My grandmother and I would play the alphabet game and try to locate every letter from *a* to *z* in road signs. There were no car seats for kids, and using the seat belt was unheard of. Nowadays, the kids are strapped in tighter than the crew of a space shuttle. I have even considered putting helmets on them in the car. It makes perfect sense to me, and with the popularity of NASCAR, I'm sure it would become socially acceptable in no time. We could have a pit crew who could refill sippy cups in ten seconds flat. Our sponsors would be Pampers, Kraft Foods, and Prozac.

With my kids, the traveling alphabet game keeps them entertained only to the letter *b*, so we put a movie in the DVD player. Once the kids start getting tired of endless movies, we resort to a mangled version of the quiet game. This is something parents invented, thinking it would trick the kids into a game-type environment where they would actually be quiet. Wrong. The quiet game never works, and in order to get some peace, the stakes get higher with each hour on the road. I'll say to them, "Kids, if you guys are quiet for the next twenty minutes, we'll stop and get Icees at the next gas station." Well, they are quiet for about thirty seconds, and they still get the Icee. What a deal for them. By the time hour four rolls around, I have promised them a villa in Tuscany if I can have just five minutes of no talking. So now they have Icees, candy, stuffed animals, new bicycles, and a villa in Tuscany. Are they quiet? No! We also have battles with air temperature. Whining, one will say, "Mommy, I'm freezing!" The other one pipes in with "Mommy, I am too hot!" I know, honey. Believe me, it is hell for me, too.

Yes, my childhood days in Florida were definitely the good ol' days. No sunscreen, no high-rise condominiums blocking the view, and no shark attacks to my knowledge. Times are different, and the scenery has changed, but one thing remains constant—pure, unadulterated fun for everyone in the sun and sand. I wish I could capture the joy children experience on a daily basis. Life seems so fast and so stressed these days, but the beach brings me as close to that feeling as anything. Watching my son feel the water recede around his sinking little toes while he shrieks with excitement brings tears to my eyes. PMS had something to do with it too, but, all in all, it was a wonderful moment.

Another fun beach activity for me, albeit a little mischievous, is people watching. This is truly one of my favorite things to do, and I can do it incognito under my hat and sunglasses. In the course of an hour, I see all types of people. Older men in Speedos with deep tans and pinky rings walking alone. College girls with tight tummies, tattoos, and belly rings, who have obviously never birthed children. The preteens can be spotted a mile away with their bright, airbrushed T-shirts. I really want a shirt that reads, "Say no to shirts decorated with neon paint and compressed air." My name would be in bubble letters, of course.

Then there are the Superdads. You know the ones who have boogie boards, Nerf balls, Frisbees, multi-layered kites, and tents set up better than an Eagle Scout. I get exhausted watching them and their poor children build the next

Frank Lloyd Wright sandcastle. Notice, I have not used the term Supermom yet. This is because all moms are Supermoms at the beach. We pack, haul, entertain, apply, wipe, comfort, feed, kiss, swaddle, brush, applaud, hydrate, watch, suck in, and smile. We are freely willing to get sand in our suits, and we are happy with never reading a book again in our lifetime.

As a physical therapist, I cannot help but analyze and try to recognize ailments on unsuspecting beachgoers. Look at that guy, he obviously has a rotated hip and a leg-length discrepancy; and look at her posture, she has taken on the shape of her chair. If I lived there, I would open a beachside back-pain tiki hut, and I could get paid with sand dollars. Superdad may need me after all his activities. I could advertise with one of the Cessna airplanes pulling a banner that reads, "Conch your head? Come sea me—I can kelp!" I know it is a hard shell, but I think it would work. If they didn't get any results, they could always see a sturgeon. Sorry, I did that on porpoise.

One might think after reading all the above that the Barzenicks spend the entire day at the beach. Wrong again. About twenty minutes into setting up our little haven, the kids are ready for the pool. So we schlep all the stuff except for the sand buckets to the pool. Now another round of setting up begins. We inflate floaties, apply more sunscreen, and adjust goggles. Kids just cannot swim without goggles. If we forget the goggles, widespread panic occurs. I do not ever recall using goggles as a kid. I opened my eyes underwater, and by mid-July, I was conditioned to the searing pain in my corneas from the chlorine. My bloodshot eyes were also a nice complement to my favorite red polka-dotted swimsuit. Come to think of it, maybe those were not polka dots …

Chapter 14

Mr. Clean Genes

Mommy's little helper. No, I am not referring to the narcotic used to treat desperate housewives, but that's an idea. I am referring to my little girl, who wants to help with everything. She sees Mommy obsessively clean, wipe, sweep, and sanitize. This is probably not a good thing, but it is something to discuss in therapy when she's older. My son is even going around the house closing all the doors. My poor children. God bless them.

At Christmas, my daughter wanted a Barbie vacuum, a housekeeping cart, and real Windex. I didn't want to spoil her, so she did not get the housekeeping cart. Having inherited my clean gene, my sweetie thought it was perfectly normal to want a bottle of Oxyclean instead of a Bratz doll. After attending a local production of the *Nutcracker* ballet, she wanted to know who was going to clean up the stage after the "snowfall." "Good question, honey—maybe they can borrow our Swiffer broom." I am so glad she got the real meaning of the story.

Having a child who likes to clean sounds great, doesn't it? Well, she likes to work on things that are not high up on my priority list. She likes to clean the chalkboard easel, scrub graffiti off her baby doll's forehead, and vacuum crumbs that she purposely threw down so she could vacuum them up. Maybe she will be a door-to-door salesman or an infomercial guru one day.

In order to actually clean up, my house must be free and clear of children. It is amazing how fast a woman can move without kids at her feet. I move seamlessly from room to room, completing one chore after the next, singing, "I can bring home the bacon, fry it up in the … microwave." This must be what it feels like to clean heaven. Then, the kids come home. I don't believe they actually went to the park. They met up with a radical, covert group of toddlers who helped plot the demise of sparkling floors and fingerprintless countertops. They thrive on chaos and the element of surprise. Their Web site describes in detail the supplies needed to dismantle the Tupperware cabinet. Hidden in the crayon writings on the wall is a map to the secret headquarters. Don't let their sweet smiles and fluttering eyelashes fool you.

I do have to trade one mess for the next in order to get something done around the house. While cleaning the kitchen, I'll allow the kids to occupy themselves with Play-Doh or some other type of messy craft while sitting at their play table. They do have to wear art smocks, gloves, and gas masks. They look like government workers who have been assigned to quarantine an outbreak of mad-cow disease. And finger painting has a cubist appeal to it when done wearing surgical gloves. One mess cleaned up, another one to go. I find myself overly obsessed with cleaning supplies in the grocery-store aisle and storage-solution catalogs. Doesn't beat the shoe obsession, but what could?

Sometimes I feel like all I do is pick up and clean up. I finish one project only to turn around and find a leaking sippy cup of milk on my freshly mopped floor or my sunglasses swirling in the toilet. If it is possible to wear a hole in ceramic tile, then there will be one in front of my sink where I spend a good portion of my days.

My children know how to push my buttons. Unfortunately, my son also knows how to push the buttons on appliances, DVD players, and computer keyboards. He has managed to wash a few loads in the dishwasher but on the "pots and pans" setting. So much for Grandma's china. He has reprogrammed the TV to only show the Disney Channel and has hacked in to the Toys-R-Us Web site. I wonder if Bill Gates was a messy child?

Chapter 15

Swimming Pools, Movie Stars

It is hard to believe that summer is halfway over. It seems like it was just yesterday that I was welcoming the warm air, the brilliant sunshine, and a colorful new swimsuit. Now, I am seeking the shelter of air-conditioned environments, ice cream, and grandma underwear. With all the running around that we've been doing, I can't seem to cool off. We have had a busy summer between various camps, visiting the library, Bible school, swimming lessons, and gymnastics. I am on an infinite quest to keep the children active and to keep them from using the words that cut through me like a knife …

"We're bored," my children tell me.

"Bored? How can you be bored with all the toys, games, and movies you have? When I was little, we were never bored! We read books, chased butterflies, and spent our entire day outside discovering nature. Besides, do you know how lucky you are to even have a house to say you are bored in! There are children in other countries that live in huts without running water, electricity, and television. The children do not have any toys to play with—only a tangle of tumbleweed that rolls by the hut on a windy day. And guess what? Those children never complain!" I rant.

My daughter, the spokesperson, responds with, "But, Mommy, you won't let us go outside without our subcutaneous computer chip that tracks our location, remember?"

Oh, yeah, honey, good point. So you are bored, eh?

To avoid the negative emotion I feel associated with the boredom of others, we've been doing our share of swimming, movie watching, and eating out. I seem to be caught on a merry-go-round of crystal blue pools, 3-D theaters, and kid-friendly restaurants. *The Beverly Hillbillies* theme incessantly rings in my head: "swimming pools, movie stars ..." Cue up the trailing banjo sound. And no, we haven't been to the Blue Ridge Mountains yet. For certain, at the beginning of summer, I felt like Miss Ellie, bikini ready, tidy feet, and shiny blond locks. Spring was my renaissance period. But now, I'm starting to look and feel more like Granny (minus the shotgun)—cranky and wrinkled, my hair in a bun, and swigging moonshine. Well, diet green tea. Moonshine, I wish.

If I were to give my kids one choice of an activity, they would definitely choose swimming. Both of them love the pool and could stay in it all day if I would let them. This is where our problem begins. I seem to lose all of my power when they are in the pool. When it comes time to leave, I give them a ten-minute warning. "Children, you have ten minutes before it is time to go." I say it very calmly, clearly, and ever so politely for the benefit of other adults at the pool. Well, ten minutes turns into twenty, and I tell them with a little less ease in my voice, "You've had ten extra minutes, and now it is time to get out. So, please get out." I am completely ignored. Their little goggles must be on too tight, cutting off circulation to their ears. I take a deep breath, gather my thoughts, and decide to flank them. The other side of the pool may bring me more luck. A better vantage point awaits me at the ladder. I say it again, but sternly and staggered this time, "It. Is. Time. To. Go. Get. Out. *Now*." My son gets the message, and he makes his way to the side of the pool. I lift him out and say, "Good boy." I realize I've just praised him for not listening to me. Oh well. Now for the big sister.

As soon as my lips start to speak, she dives underwater and zips away. A delinquent mermaid, that girl. At this point, I am about to unleash the fury. The temperature outside does not compete with my internal heat. I am ready to pull a Moses on her. Part the seas, I promise. If she could only see that under my sunglasses are laser-beam eyes directed at her glistening body. She begins to smell fear and swims toward me to climb out. By now, ten minutes has turned into thirty minutes, and she is still trying to negotiate, but this time the unit of measurement has changed to a number of jumps. "Just three more jumps, Mommy!" I then hear giggles from others, and I turn around to find my son naked and peeing on an azalea bush. She takes this opportunity to jump in *again*. After corralling my son, the streaker, I squat down very close to the side, remove my sunglasses, and give *the look*, followed by the clenched-teeth talk. She gets out quickly. I then swear to them we are never going back swimming if they choose to ignore me at the pool.

I guess I can understand. I think back to when I was little; swimming was my favorite summer activity, too. Remember, we didn't have goggles. Red eyes were like a badge of courage—daring chlorine to irritate them. Diving boards were also in fashion, and the community pool where I used to swim had a high diving board. I was six years old, thirty feet in the air, and more slippery than a Valdez seal, but nothing ever happened to me. I made it through just fine.

Nowadays, my kids swim only in the shallow water and with flotation devices that could support a lunar-module ocean landing. My son looks like the Michelin man in his built-in floating swimsuit. He doesn't really float, he bobs. Picture a really cute and lovable dinghy—that's him.

There are days when I just do not feel like taking them swimming. First of all, I never get in the pool. As a matter of fact, I never see any other moms swimming, either. There is of course the bathing-suit issue. I mean, once you've given birth, things are, so to speak, rearranged. Perky areas become droopy. Smaller areas become *large,* and high areas become lowwww. Then, there is the hairdo. We certainly don't want those highlights turning green, now do we? Of course, we don't like getting cold. When I do get in the pool or the ocean for that matter, my upper half remains completely dry. I feel like a paper towel in a Bounty commercial. Dipped halfway in a blue liquid, and I still come out pliable and soft.

So, when they are begging to swim day after day, I have to come up with a few outs. Sometimes I tell them that fresh chemicals are in the pool, and it is closed for the day. Other times, I'll say that a storm is coming or I just saw lightning in the distance. Then, there are the piranhas ...

My husband, Jay, does save me a lot. The pool definitely brings out the boy in him, and he will gladly get in the pool with our kids, shoot water guns, do handstands, and judge my daughter's cannonballs. The cannonball—every kid knows it and wants to master it.

I've decided that maybe I should give in to the green hair, expose a few stretch marks, and get completely wet. As a matter of fact, the next time my kids give me trouble and swim away from me when it is time to get out of the pool, I am going to jump in and get them!

Chapter 16

Hail Mary

The countdown to school starting again is ticking in my head. Ten, nine, eight, seven, six, five, four, *free!* I am *so* ready for a routine to begin again. I feel out of sync, suspended in a time-space continuum of swimming pools, Popsicles, and matinees. We plan our days as well as a couple of hippies traveling across the country in a Volkswagen van—no structure, lots of protests, and dirty matted hair. I'll call it the Age of Aquariums, Aquariums, yeah …

You see, we have sought out every tourist attraction in the southeast in a futile attempt to entertain the children. Boy, are they a tough crowd to please. We visited water parks, city parks, state parks, and even Rosa Parks. We've watched dolphins perform, seals clap, snakes slither, and rhinos graze. I've actually done a lot of grazing myself this summer on leftover chicken nuggets, Cheetos, and popcorn. If I keep it up, I'll soon have my own atmosphere that the kids can visit next summer.

Being a military history buff (who knew?) and a patriotic citizen, I once again planned to take the kids to see the USS *Alabama* battleship in Mobile on our way home from Florida. As always, I approach the bridge with honest intentions, but I just can't seem to veer the car off the exit when we are making such good time. We blow by it at seventy-five-plus miles an hour and tell the kids to look out the window quickly. Unfortunately, they now think a battleship is a beat-up red Yugo with a California license plate that is emitting blue exhaust and has a bumper sticker that reads, "Save the Earth,

Stop Global Warming." I even think I saw the driver throw a clove cigarette out the window. Darn hippies!

Whenever we are home and not seeking outside sources of entertainment, I have to hear repetitive phrases like "I have nothing to do" and "I want to play with someone." My daughter can be with a friend all day, come home, and not five minutes later, want someone else to play with.

"Mommy, can I play with Sarah?" she asks.

"Honey, Sarah is gone on vacation," I'll say.

"What about Peyton?" she continues.

"She is at gymnastics today," I patiently reply.

"Call Caroline, I want her," she impatiently replies.

"Sweetie, she is at summer camp," I say.

Frustrated, she starts firing off names like a Tommy gun, leaving all adverbs and sentence structure behind. I do the same.

"Frankie?" she asks.

"Fishing," I say.

"Lily?" she asks.

"Moved," I rapidly declare.

"Mackie?" she says with a defeated tone.

"Seaside," I say, followed by, "Babe, just give up."

She goes through the entire roster of kids from school, and I have to keep coming up with stories on their whereabouts. I get so desperate, I could sometimes settle for her playing with the Bates twins. You know their dad, Norman.

Sometimes, pulling out the art supplies buys us some time. My little boy loves to color. His artwork is more along the Jackson Pollock style. Actually, if you look under his highchair, original masterpieces are being formed with yesterday's lunch. A little splash of juice, a few corn kernels, and a smattering of strawberry jelly—wow, he is an artist, indeed!

With all of their drawings and paintings, I would need a separate building to house the collection. But what do I do? I filter out the good ones and put them in their respective keepsakes boxes. Discreetly and chocked full of mommy guilt, I send the other ones to the trashcan when the kids aren't looking. I bury them under coffee grounds or some other undesirable waste, ensuring they will not be discovered.

So, with the end of summer near, I begin to imagine the faint chimes of the school bell ringing. What a beautiful sound. I anticipate August 21 like a child anticipates Santa's arrival. The uniforms, monogrammed book sack, and sparkling-white Keds are lined up, ready to be filled with my kindergartner. Carpool, here we come. I think I'll just slow the car down to a crawl and have her perform the tuck-and-roll stunt out the door that we've been practicing this summer. It gives new meaning to a Catholic school jumper. Brush it off, honey, I'll see you at 2:30!

Chapter 17

Premature Empty-Nest Syndrome

The day that I was anxiously awaiting finally arrived—August 21, the first day of kindergarten for my daughter. I had been anticipating the start of school for weeks and was completely caught off guard by my emotions that morning. I was excited but nervous. I had stomach flutters and was feeling and looking a bit like a mother grizzly—I wanted my cub to venture out but was ready to pounce, if needed.

Much to my surprise, my daughter did not have any trouble getting up early, putting on her uniform, or brushing her hair. I immediately thought that something had gone awry—I mean, this is the kid that cried for weeks in preschool, the one I had to offer bribes every morning in order to get her dressed. The entire summer, she was in total denial about ever having to start school again. When I would ask her, "Honey, are you looking forward to starting kindergarten?" all I got back in return was, "Can we talk about something else?" I was worried, let me tell you.

Now something was different about her—she was cooperative, pleasantly polite, and had a sparkle in her eye. She also requested bran cereal and fruit for breakfast. Interesting. The Pop-Tarts were so disappointed. Not only did she brush her teeth for the entire two minutes, using a gentle, circular motion, but she also wanted to floss. Strange. Was she really an android whose program was set to initiate at 0600 hours on 21Aug06? Was she scanning me like the Terminator? Was that sparkle in her eye really a sparkle, or was it a high-powered laser? Did she come from the past to change the future? Was I in the Matrix? Do I need antipsychotic medication? Probably.

I knew to give up on the robot theory when she asked me to put her hair in hot rollers. This was my girl talking—she wanted to look beautiful for the first day of school. This was where the tears began for me, and it wasn't because I burned my finger on a roller. Which I did. My little baby, my precious first child is leaving me! She is in *school.* Real school. All-day school. What have I done!

From that point on, I was a basket case. I was borderline weepy, and I was trying to hide it from her. She was strong and confident and couldn't wait to get to school. They must have promised her candy, I know it.

As we pulled out of the driveway ahead of schedule, I caught a glimpse of her in the rearview mirror. The warm, morning light caught her face, and I realized how grown up she looked. Those big brown eyes, those perfect curls (thank you very much). She looked crisp and spit-shined.

We pulled up to the school with me holding back tears and taking very deep breaths. On the contrary, my daughter was bouncy, anxious, and alive with wonder. I looked around the campus and felt at home. This was my school growing up, and it was comfortable to me. All the buildings seemed much smaller than I remembered, though. I saw a few other parents who were my classmates walking their kids to school, and I saw my seventh-grade teacher, Mrs. Wagner, still smiling and greeting everyone like it was her first year of teaching.

As we entered the kindergarten classroom, the teachers welcomed my baby girl with big hugs and warm smiles. I could tell immediately that they loved her and would take care of her. The classroom was so inviting, organized, and centered. My obsessive-compulsive inner self was delighted to find that everything was lined up perfectly and color coordinated. I wanted to stay!

Then, in a cruel turn of events, the teacher decided to read the book *The Kissing Hand* to all the children and parents. Was my face not blotchy enough already? Must she read a heartwarming tale about the first day of school for a little raccoon to put me into full-blown hysterics? Tears were streaming, but I kept the unattractive heaving to a minimum. I looked around. Good, other mommies were crying, too. Moms who had three children or more were the only ones with a sly grin, an even complexion, and crystal clear corneas.

The time had come to leave her, and I knew there would be prying of hands off legs. As she shook me off of her, I lunged for the teacher's leg. She politely asked me to stop, but I would not go down that easy. The last thing I remember was a swift whack with a ruler coupled with a mild electrical shock.

OK, I will leave now. Too bad my daughter's name is not Stella, because that is what I would have been screaming down the hallway.

So, I guess this is where it all begins for my little one. She will make friends that will last a lifetime and experience learning in a wonderfully nurturing environment. As I exited the school, I knew a piece of me was in that kindergarten classroom. A fingernail, to be exact, that was broken during the struggle. I felt calm and at peace knowing she is in wonderful hands.

Chapter 18

My First Ectomy

Here I sit at my computer after a one-month-long hiatus from writing, exercising, and eating out. I have felt like a kid again over the month of August. I've eaten Popsicles, stayed in bed until 11:00 a.m., and even had my mom kiss me on the forehead and take care of me. If you are wondering about my recent regression into childhood, I will share. The reason? I had a tonsillectomy. Yes, after many decades of quietly inhabiting the back of my throat, my tonsils began to protest. So, under general anesthesia I went. In addition to the thought of scalpels slicing and sutures tying, having to undergo anesthesia brought its own share of anxiety. I worried about the anesthesia not working properly and, even worse, working too much. I pictured the surgeon coming out of the operating room, head hanging while approaching my husband to tell him, "I am sorry. She didn't make it. It was a simple tonsillectomy, but her body couldn't handle it." Ridiculous thoughts, I know. On a regular basis, my brain likes to take ordinary scenarios and turn them into epic tales of misadventure.

Aside from worrying about the anesthesia, I knew I would feel more comfortable with the surgery if I had a manicure, pedicure, eyebrow waxing, bikini waxing, and smooth skin. So I buffed, shaved, exfoliated, cleansed, toned, peeled, and plucked most of my exposed body parts. I mean, if I didn't make it through the surgery, at least I would look good for my final exit into the afterlife. "Gee, how sad, but did you see how *well groomed* she was?" I would be grinning proudly while my spirit hovered above my peaceful body. Vanity over rationale, I always say.

At my pre-op appointment, my doctor told me to expect a difficult recovery. No sugar coating here. She said that when adults have their tonsils out, it is very painful and takes about three weeks to fully recover. Children recover within days and usually do not remember the procedure at all. Well, I was in denial over the whole thing. I just knew that I would be the exception, and I would not have the pain I was warned about.

The morning of the surgery, I was starving, of course. Remember, no food or drink after midnight, and you should know, I am the ultimate rule-follower. My surgery was scheduled for late morning, and I wondered how I would possibly make it that long without eating or drinking! I prepared breakfast for the kids all the while drooling over their cinnamon rolls. My husband was sipping a cup of freshly brewed Community coffee, and all I could enjoy was the little bit of moisture I savored while brushing my teeth. When it was finally time to leave for the hospital, I was so hungry and parched that even the mustard in the door of my refrigerator appealed to me like it was a big, juicy, rib-eye steak. I could never make it on one of those survivor reality shows. This girl has got to eat.

I kissed my kids good-bye and told them that Mommy would be home later, but I would have a big boo-boo in my throat. I explained that I would be very sleepy and would be in bed for a few days, but they could still snuggle with me. "Will you be able to yell?" was the only question my daughter had for me.

At the hospital, we checked in, and I was admitted into the same-day surgery unit. Same day. You go in, they take parts out, and you leave. Sounds easy. I had to wait a few hours, and by 10:30 I was ready to tackle anyone that walked by with a mere cracker crumb in his or her pocket. Conveniently, my husband brought a few snacks—for him. As he munched loudly on a peanut butter granola bar, my last shout, my tonsils' last hoorah was loaded in the cylinder, ready to fire. Lucky for him, the operating-room assistant came in to get me just in time. Seeing "tonsillectomy" on the schedule, I think he was expecting to pick up a five-year-old child. Not only was I not five, I could easily have been his mother. I arrived in the staging area where the anesthesiologist and nurse anesthetist visited with me. They administered the "happy" drugs, and after that, I remember nothing.

About an hour later, I woke up in recovery feeling nauseated, disoriented, and jittery. Then, I swallowed. Someone told me before the surgery, "You've given birth twice; you can handle pain just fine." Well, at that moment, I felt like I had given birth to twins but through my mouth! I then made a decision to never swallow again. I would invest in Kleenex and discreetly pretend as though I was dabbing my lipstick. I guess I'll have to buy lipstick now.

After leaving the recovery room, I was aggravated with myself that I didn't learn the sign for "morphine." I taught both of my children sign language, but how could I have left out such an important reference to a proven narcotic! I'll be prepared next time. My sweet husband greeted me in the hallway and asked me, "Hey, honey, how are you feeling?" Shouldn't he know that his words were even hard to swallow?

I was told that I would have to drink and pee before I left to go home. I'm not sure they realized the stubborn fe*mule* they were dealing with. Drink something? Are they insane? My throat feels like Freddy Krueger assisted in the operating room. And *get up*? I just had minor outpatient surgery, and they expect me to walk? Stretchers have wheels for a reason, and I planned on using one for the next week or so. Well, hours passed, but the urine didn't. I knew I would have to drink in order to get things flowing. The nice nurse brought me a few ice chips to start with. Hospital ice is so good—the perfect consistency of crunch and size. I let the ice melt on my tongue, but I was afraid to swallow it. I desperately wished I were on the "Next Day" or the "Whenever You Feel like Going Home" surgery unit, if indeed one existed. Everyone was ready to go home but me. The nurse, my husband, and even the janitor were waiting on me to drink as if they were watching a baseball in the outfield waiting to be caught. "There it goes … she's looking up … her head's tilting back … she's going for it … there it is!" They were shouting "Hooray!" while I was wondering why I was drinking chilled puree of thumb tacks. It was going to be a long three weeks.

Fast forward one week after surgery. The kids knew I couldn't scream or yell, and they took advantage of it. I learned to reprimand them by hastily writing words down on a notepad. I used an extra fat Sharpie marker for emphasis. Too bad my son can't read yet.

As the days dragged on, eating was still a struggle. Swallowing is one of those automatic motions that happens often but one that can be easily taken for granted. (You just consciously swallowed, didn't you?) Every time I attempted to swallow, I felt like I was a fire-breathing dragon who backfires or I was dining on filet of porcupine. Better yet, a sword swallower with a tremor. It was rough, let me tell you. Then came the scabs. And I'm not talking about antiunion workers here. I have noticed the older I get, the more apt I am to discuss physical ailments with people. I find myself telling anyone who will listen about my surgery. I mean, I'm writing an entire chapter dedicated to it. When I mention the six stitches in my throat, I feel oddly validated when others respond, "ew." Discussing hemorrhoids, rashes, arthritis, polyps, and "suspicious" moles is common ground among adults over forty. Instead of being in a book club or a coffee klatch, maybe I should start a Goiters Guild or a Fungus Federation. I'm sure many folks would be itching to join!

Chapter 19

It Must Be the Lead

Kids these days just don't know how good they have it. Everything is available at their fingertips whenever they want it. I feel like I enable this to happen because I use bribery on a regular basis. If you let me do this, I'll give you that. Give, give, give and they take, take, take. And we let them.

As a parent, I feel it is my responsibility to teach my children how tough life was growing up for me. For example, I actually had to use a phone with a cord, mind you. The phone weighed about thirty pounds and came with a top-of-the-line rotary dial. My index finger is now overdeveloped thanks to using the rotary phone at Grandma's house. Researchers should look into arthritic conditions in the elderly, and I'll bet they could find a correlation between rotary phone usage and crooked fingers.

Caller ID is a technology that our kids take for granted. Oh, how I wish I could travel back in time to high school with caller ID. I know it was some tortured genius who was picked on in school that invented caller ID. His life's journey was to figure out who put Prince Albert in a can. Bullies and mean girls must have been devastated when this invention came out.

Another thing that made life tough in my childhood was an extinct piece of equipment that we used our legs to power. You may recall its name … does "bicycle" ring a bell? Mine had a long banana seat with embedded sparkly glitter in it and a lovely flower basket on the front. My, how times have changed. The other day, I saw a few kids riding battery-charged scooters while talking on their cell phones. Have we lost the fun of carefree bike riding with our friends? By the time my son reaches eight or nine years old, he will probably have a hovercraft skateboard and a cell phone microchip implanted into his temple for hands-free operation!

I really am trying to teach my kids the value of money and how blessed they are to have food, shelter, and love. I've had visions of taking them to nursing homes to brighten an elderly person's day, an animal shelter to adopt an unwanted pet, and a soup kitchen to serve the homeless a hot meal. Instead, we always end up at Target. My car automatically heads to that store; we just sit back and enjoy the ride. If Big Brother was tracking my car, chances are, the beep on the screen would be located at a Target parking lot. No mystery there.

Enjoying nature and the outdoors has also become a challenge for this generation. When I was growing up, my parents had to beg me to come inside. We played outside all day, only coming in for grape Kool-Aid and pasty sandwiches made from white bread. That was straight up, real Kool-Aid with real sugar—imagine that. I don't think we ever wore shoes and could walk across gravel, stickers, and hot cement without blinking an eye. Nowadays, Berber carpet is even rough on my feet.

We had mosquito bites from head to toe, and our mothers applied the orange, iridescent Mercurochrome to soothe the itch. Merthiolate was another topical medicine that looked the same but burned like fire when applied. Or was it the other way around? I can't remember because the mercury poisoning from the product has destroyed my memory. What was I just saying?

My kids do get a dose of the outdoors when we walk from the house to the car to go places. Let's hope that is enough sunlight for vitamin D synthesis. They have also watched the movies *Madagascar* and *The Jungle Book* numerous times. That's enough nature, right? They must think of a forest like a distant land, unconquered and uncharted. They must dream of visiting this "foreign" place one day.

I do have fantasies of moving the whole family to Montana, away from it all. No television, no cell phones, no PlayStations, only acres and acres of beautiful pasture with horses. My kids could raise little chicks and rabbits, and I could ring a dinner bell when the biscuits and gravy were ready. We could live like *Little House on the Prairie* or the Amish or something. I would not have to put makeup on or do my hair—not that I do that now, but it is a nice thought. My upper-body workout would consist of throwing bales of hay, delivering newborn calves, and using the lasso to wrangle that pesky, stray mustang. My lower-body workout would involve pushing the clutch on the John Deere bush hog and squatting down to milk the cows at 5:00 a.m.

Forgive me for daydreaming. I guess I need to snap out of it, because I don't think rural Montana has any Target stores.

Chapter 20

Five Little Monkeys

What makes a toddler tick? As I observe my son move about the house, I definitely see parallels to creatures of the wild. I think of myself as a stay-at-home Jane Goodall of sorts. I study my primates diligently while folding clothes or doing the dishes. Yes, my home has dangers just as the Congo. My little subjects, under careful watch, scale the suburban jungle of bookshelves, cabinets, and bureau drawers.

My son has a particular affinity for my neatly arranged, Dewey-decimalized book collection. He loves to dismantle the books one by one, large hardcovers to small paperbacks. Titles such as *What to Expect from a One-Year-Old, 1-2-3 Discipline, Don't Sweat the Small Stuff,* and his personal favorite, *Discover Your Inner Child* end up torn and tattered, with one corner eaten for good measure. Some end up completely coverless. I guess those weren't so tasty. He seems to know the ones that apply to him and seeks to destroy any information that would allow his mother to have a leg up.

Aside from the deepest love imaginable and the completeness that my children have given me, they have also taught me important lessons on letting go and accepting less. In 2000 BC (before children), my home could be visited at any hour of the day without any apologies. Today visitors have to endure stepping over small but colorful plastic Lego land mines, one-eyed dolls with chopped-up hair, and an errant spoon with dried peanut butter lying around. That is just in the foyer. *Please sign the following disclaimer before entering the bathroom:*

> *I hereby release the Barzenicks from an injury incurred while removing the potty seat from the toilet, stubbing one toe or any subsequent digits on the kiddy stool, and any psychological trauma due to the overwhelming SpongeBob décor plastered from wall to wall.*

My children continue to teach me many things, sentimental and scientific. For a little chemistry lesson, did you know that Cheetos residue on fingertips coupled with a runny nose have the adhesive properties of superglue? I'll bet you didn't know that dry-erase markers permanently stain clothing. This makes no sense considering you can wipe them off a board with just your fingertip. I have bought every washable marker known to man, but the kids gravitate to the Sharpies and the dry-erase markers. I have stock in Mr. Clean Magic Erasers.

I have finally accepted that every room in the house shows evidence that children live here. Even the driveway has a stray ball on it that has been deflated and faded by the sun. It is starting to look good there, anthill and all. The area of the house where I like to escape at times, my sanctuary, my big bathtub, has a naked Barbie floating in it. Or at least my husband wished it did. The beautiful lanai is now called the "play porch." Teak lounge chairs are replaced with puffy plastic kids' furniture. I have managed to feng shui the Dora the Explorer play kitchen, though. My daughter says that since I moved it facing north and painted one burner brick red, she can really feel good energy coming from it.

I have decided that there will be days when I will simply choose not to clean up, pick up, or wipe up anything. I am reminded while looking around my house that I would not trade having kids stuff for anything in the world. It means family. It means joy. It means being blessed every day.

Chapter 21

Heaven Only Knows

One of my favorite things to read in the *Reader's Digest* is the "Quotable Quotes" section. Every blue moon, I actually get to curl up and read something other than *Brown Bear, Brown Bear* or the directions on a microwaveable dinner. I look forward to reading the poignant, funny, and memorable quotes by interesting and sometimes surprising people. When I can't get to the *Reader's Digest*, I can always count on my daughter for a few good quotable quotes of her own.

Hers can be poignant too but are usually funny and definitely memorable. She has always amazed me with her unique insight into the world around her. At age three, she saw a story on working dogs that featured a German shepherd who was a police dog. With her head tilted a little to the side and with a curious but cynical look she asked, "Mommy, how do police dogs handcuff people?"

Sometimes her questions or quotes are not so cute. For example, when I was pregnant with my son and could easily pass for a blond Beluga whale, she said, "Mommy, did you know your butt is growing big, just like your belly?" Thanks for the brutal honesty.

Some of her questions are spiritually based and quite profound. While riding in the car, out of the blue she asked, "Why did God make life?" Since I wasn't near the computer to Google that question, I did the best I could with my answer. Fumbling with my words, I told her that we are here because he loves us and wants us to love what he created. After a few minutes of absorbing what I had said, she asked, "Then why do you say you hate wasps and raw oysters? God created those things, Mommy!" Somebody get me a search engine, and quick!

Another time, we were attending my niece, Jai-Li's, baptism. Out loud, in church, mind you, she blurts, "Why is that man washing her hair?" Fortunately, the parishioners around us had a sense of humor, as did the priest.

Lately, she has developed a hint of sassiness and defiance toward me. I am hoping it is a stage she is going through. I look at old pictures of her and remember how perfectly sweet she was from morning until night. No talking back, no tantrums, no attitude. On a particularly challenging evening, I reminded her of those days. In a long-winded monologue that only a mother could project, I told her, "Honey, do you remember when you were two and Mommy could do no wrong? You were always hugging me and wanted me near you all of the time. You didn't sass me or say anything ugly." She matter-of-factly replied, "Well, that is because I couldn't talk yet." Good point. It makes me wonder what my son is thinking these days.

Speaking of my son, when I was teaching him baby sign language, my daughter liked to be involved and would try to help him make the signs. One afternoon, when he was being especially noisy she told me, "Mom, we need a sign for 'Shut up, baby!'" I couldn't help but chuckle at that one.

I do have to say that she can be very sweet with some of her quotable quotes. Last year, our beloved dog, Dixie, died of cancer. My little girl was devastated and had some interesting questions about dying, death, and heaven. Our thoughtful neighbors gave us a rose bush to plant in Dixie's honor.

When she was watering it one afternoon, she told me, "You know, Mom, Dixie is going to dig a hole in the clouds with her paws so she can see her roses from heaven." That one brought tears to my eyes, but then I got a giggle out of her next statement: "I wonder if Jesus has dog food for her in heaven."

"Well, sure he does, and I'll bet it is the *Christian* Science Diet brand," I told her.

Ignoring my pun, she asked, "Does *he* feed her, or do the angels?"

"They take turns, honey. You could learn from that, you know," I replied, interjecting a lesson in sharing.

"But where do they buy the dog food?" she said.

Satisfying her curiosity, I replied, "Wal-Mart."

I imagine that the entrance to the Pearly Gates is the ultimate check-out line.

Children are natural comedians and philosophers, and if we really listen to them, they can teach us a thing or two. Who knows what my daughter will come up with next. Just the other day, she told me that she wants pink hair with a few purple stripes when she grows up. Uh-oh.

Chapter 22

Thumb-Suckers Anonymous

Ah, motherhood. Is there a job that is any harder? Rattlesnake wrestler? Navy SEAL? Double Agent? Both kids are sick, and according to the doctor, they are "sharing the same bacteria." Who knew they could share? I consider this challenge as an experiment of sorts. Will precise distribution of the medicine and careful observation of my little subjects prove any statistical significance? Let's discuss the control group, a.k.a. the parents, newly defined as the not-really-in-control group.

Vigorous hand washing, better than most surgeons I might add, has obviously not been enough for these little hands. Not even the "guess this bacteria" flash-card drill has sunk in. I knew I should have started this when they were in the womb. You know, a captive audience. Much to my chagrin, the children continue to touch public surfaces, and, worst of all, other children's hands! Then the point of entry occurs, the route of contamination, so to speak—thumb-sucking! Yes, both of my children are chronic thumb-suckers. They have the constant been-in-the-tub-too-long look to their opposable digits. One might think there is a hole at the end of the thumb that offers an endless supply of their favorite beverage. I've had to establish savings accounts for future orthodontist bills as well as for the psychotherapy that will be needed for their mother's obsession with every germ in the universe and its half-life on doorknobs.

Getting two children to take separate medicines for eyes, ears, nose, and throat three times a day is certainly challenging. I have used Santa, shots, and suckers, not always in that particular order, to bribe them into taking their medicine. Maybe they can discuss that in therapy one day as well.

This illness of the month has involved all of the senses—ears, eyes, nose, mouth, and thumbs, of course. Both kids have coughs that sound like they have been smoking unfiltered Camels for fifty years. Even the doctor suggested the low-tar brand. When they cough, people freeze in their tracks and stare like we are a group of oozing lepers. That look always elicits a response from me, completely truthful, when I say, "Oh, it's just their sinuses." It is amazing how we justify a "sinus drip" when really our offspring are a bunch of little Typhoid Marys running around. Why should we create panic among the masses? Just smile and say S-I-N-U-S-E-S. Ah, everyone feel better now?

Chapter 23

Wisdom, Teeth

I recently attended the Christening ceremony of our dear friend's new baby girl, Claire. She was so alert and so perfect, and she didn't even cry. I, however, did shed a tear or two. Watching her adoring parents beaming at her beauty, innocence, and spiritual welcoming sent my tears streaming. As I held my own little girl and reflected on her baptism, I felt a comforting warmth bubbling up from within. This time, it wasn't the Burrito Grande from the night before, but the peaceful feeling of being present and feeling a connection to everyone in the room. Our lives are so busy, so scheduled, and, at times, so centered around insignificant details that we forget that we are all part of the whole picture and our needs are, indeed, the same.

I am not sure if this perspective would have come to me at this age if children were not in my life. My children have taught and continue to teach me many things with each day that passes. I look at them as thumb-sucking minimonks who always have a message for me hidden in the obvious. Aside from the patience, kindness, and understanding they have taught me, I have also learned that square pegs do fit in round holes if you gnaw one corner down with a first-year molar. I have learned that boxes and bubble wrap are more fun than any electronic toy on the market and that expensive toys are indirectly proportional to the frequency that one will play with them. My husband's Shelby Cobra is a perfect example of that. Confucius say: "Man with big engine has lots of gas." Confucius's wife say: "Man has lots of gas."

When I take my son outside, he always finds a peculiar leaf or rock that he presents to me as a gift. The lesson here is obvious—notice the Earth and what it gives us. He will also doggedly track a single ant all over the driveway while I follow behind him closely. Lesson: the old lumbar spine ain't what it used to be. When outdoors, my daughter likes to pick flowers, mostly from the neighbor's yard, but we won't tell. She hands them over to me, and by the end of our walk, I look like a very haggard bride carrying weeds for a bouquet. Technically, I am bride as well as haggard, so it is a comfortable place for me. She does expect me to keep all of her pickings, nose included. So, regardless of the variety, I display the harvest of wilted clover flowers and poison sumac in a nice vase at the kitchen sink. I do have to say, the festering rash is a good excuse not to wash the dishes.

My children see things that I do not see—they notice the beauty and detail in life. I think I used to see that, but now I have forgotten how to look. I want that detail back in my life. I want to see the tree instead of the forest, and I will continue my quest for simplicity.

Really, I would like to see things the way my kids do sometimes. Face value with no spin. This does work to my advantage at times. For example, my daughter was singing a popular song on the radio called "My Humps." I was mortified that she knew the words, and I had to intervene and offer a literal interpretation of the song. I told her the song was written about camels, in first person, of course. OK, that one worked, but then came these lyrics: "Whatcha gonna do with all that junk, all that junk inside your trunk?" Oh my goodness, this is on the radio! Heaven help our daughters. I knew the camel story was faltering, and I had better come up with a secondary explanation. Thinking fast and quickly turning off the radio, I told her that part of the song is about bringing stuff to Goodwill. The explanation worked, but what will I say to her a few years from now?

I am very concerned. There are so many unhealthy images of women out there in everything we see. But what is a parent to do? Take away television, screen books, keep her away from shopping centers and newsstands? I can certainly limit the exposure, but I think the best thing to do is to provide her with a good example of what being a woman is all about. That goes for my boy, too. Respect, confidence, independence, and self-awareness are my definitions of success. I will press forward, have faith, and openly receive the lessons given to me by my children. Leaves, flowers, or humps, I'm there.

Chapter 24

Handyman Wanted

This past week, I decided to save my husband a little money and paint the kid's bathroom myself. The "old me" used to do projects like this all of the time; never would I think I couldn't handle a simple repair job, general car maintenance, or even basic dog training. I had all of the time in the world to learn how to do such things. I invested in many do-it-yourself books like *Deck Building for Dummies, The Perfect Patio, Woodworking for Lathe-y People,* and *The Perfect Puppy.* Notice I use the word *perfect* a lot. Maybe I should be buying self-help books, too. Being the eternal pragmatist, I have to read how to do something before I start it. I did this when I was pregnant, too. Not "how to" get pregnant. I do have distant memories of that process. Distant memories, just ask my husband. Once, I read a book called *A Woman's Guide to Car Repairs.* How insulting to think women must have a special guide to take care of a car. I mean, we all know about carburetors. You should eat the low-glycemic kind, whole grains and all.

In the prechildren era of my life, I would plan to lay a cobblestone walkway, change the oil in my Jeep, and build a purple-martin birdhouse all in one weekend. Now, I am lucky if I can get around to putting makeup on the other eye before the day is through. Most things are half-finished in my house. My daughter's hair gets brushed but only on the top layer. The underside remains matted and tangled. The upside is that it keeps her warmer—a similar principle exists with Siberian Husky fur: the top layer is smooth, and the undercoat is coarse and wiry. I have to divide my tasks into small increments in order to complete them. Next week I will be able to finish brushing my molars, and the following week, if time permits, I can get to the incisors. No one told me that children take precedence over personal hygiene. It is true. Just look at the heels of your average mother. Do you remember the frozen Neanderthal woman they found in the Himalayan Mountains a few years back? Well, her feet look better than mine.

When you have kids, special projects just don't happen in a timely manner, if at all. As a matter of fact, I stopped painting the bathroom in order to write this chapter. Something about the soothing ocean color had sparked my creativity. Actually, I pretended I had to potty so my husband could watch the kids for a minute. What a woman must do for some peace. While seated, I continued to multitask. I caught up on reading the school newsletter, pushed back the cuticles on one hand, and made a few phone calls. There are a few special friends (you know who you are) that I can talk to while in the bathroom, but only an elite few get to hear the flush. This includes the cable company.

Believe it or not, the painting project is complete. It may not be perfect, but I am learning that it is all right not to be. This needs to be my mantra …

Chapter 25

New-Age Motherhood

I just returned from an incredible trip out west with my friend, Ashley. We both celebrated birthdays this week and thought it would be a great idea to travel to Sedona, Arizona, for a little R and R. We are both mothers of little children, and we both have very busy husbands who would be playing the role of Mr. Mom for the week. For me, it took about three weeks to plan to leave for five days. I used a nifty computer spreadsheet to help organize the days that I would be gone. I put every single detail into the schedule including breakfast selections, wake-up times, hair-washing nights, matching barrettes, homework overview, gymnastics schedule, physicians phone number, drug allergies, potty-training tips, bedtime-story favorites, and not forgetting the book sack. When I passed out copies to my husband, my mother, my mother-in-law, my sister-in-law, and my neighbor, they all smiled graciously, secretly thinking how over-the-top I am. I also called my daughter's teacher to tell her I would be gone and to please excuse any odd hairstyles or mismatched socks.

The Sunday morning that we left, the children were still asleep. They looked so perfect and peaceful lying there. My son was snuggled in on his stomach with his butt in the air, limbs tucked in and looking a lot like a green tree frog that sticks to the window. My daughter was cozily nestled into her stuffed animal, and her thick, brown hair flowed across the pink flowered pillowcase. I'm sure leaving them for five days had something to do with the auras around them that morning as well as the faint sound of angels singing. Mommy guilt was starting to brew. Neurosis was also creeping in as I envisioned the plane going down in a fiery crash. I could see the headlines and all.

On the airplane, we were asking ourselves, What have we done? We are leaving our babies, our sweeties! We don't deserve sleep-filled nights and uninterrupted meals. Did you hear that? Was that the engine or the wing? Well, it took all of one day and looking out at the beautiful red-rock canyons to realize that this was a great idea and our kids would be fine.

At home, however, was another story. I thought I would share the e-mail transcriptions between my husband and me during the trip. Readers, it is personal, but I'll share anyway, so here it goes.

Sunday, October 1
Dear Jay,

We just arrived in Sedona. Obviously, the plane landed safely, and I am still alive. Save these e-mails for the kids in case something happens to me while I'm gone. You know the place is teeming with coyotes, rattlesnakes, and scorpions. I'll be careful, though. How did the kids do this morning? Did you make the pancakes I suggested? Did the baby eat well? Make sure you keep the front door locked because he is starting to learn how to turn the deadbolt. Oh, and make sure our girl flosses her teeth after brushing. Her teeth are getting a bit cruddy. Please call everyone and make sure they have laminated the schedule I left for them. Oh, and how are you honey? Thanks again. I'll write soon. I love you.

Bren

Dear Bren,

I just got your e-mail. The kids are fine, they didn't even ask about you. I brought them to your mom's house, and they didn't want to leave, so I let them stay the entire day. I was able to watch football, some tennis, and the golf tournament. I hope you are having fun, don't worry about a thing. I love you, too.

Monday, October 2
Dear Jay,

Wow, this place is beautiful! It is about seventy-two degrees and sunny. No humidity either. Ashley and I are going on a hike this morning, and then we are going to do a yoga class later. How did the morning go getting our girl off to school? Don't forget she has gymnastics today. She likes the pink leotard with the velour trim. Avoid the black one because she says it is itchy. Also, don't let the baby eat in his room. I've posted the Heimlich maneuver and child rescue breathing instructions on the refrigerator. Make sure everyone reads it and initials it. I hope you have a great day. They really didn't mention me? I love you.

Me.

Dear Bren,

You didn't tell me that I have to physically remove her from the bed to get her up! Your mom came at 6:45 a.m. to help me. Thank God for her. I am starting to catch a cold. Great, just what I need. The baby had three poop diapers last night. Is that normal? Could he have e-coli? Anyway, glad you are having fun. Gotta go, the baby is screaming.

Tuesday, October 3
Dear Jay,

Happy birthday to me! Yeah! Today is my day! Our hike in the Red Rocks was incredible. We visited a sacred Native American rock formation where they celebrate summer solstice. It is quite amazing, and there is a spiritual energy resonating in the canyon. Life is good. Sorry if you've tried to call me, but cell phones do not work here. Oh, how are my babies?

Love,
Me.

Dear Bren,

Well, we had a horrible night. The baby woke up screaming around 3:00 a.m. calling "Daddy." I think he forgot about you already (just kidding). And now I'm sick. I have a sore throat and fever and had to get a shot today. Incredibly, we made it to school on time, but I sure did miss your mom this morning. The kids didn't want breakfast until it was time to walk out the door, so I gave them both a Popsicle. The box said fruit flavored, so I figured it would be all right. I forgot to put a clean diaper on the baby this morning, but I eventually figured it out when I noticed he was walking like John Wayne. My mom is coming today to watch the baby, but I guess you know that since you made the schedule. I really need to get some work done in my office. Oh, happy birthday, honey, we miss you. Believe me, we miss you.

Love,
Jay.

Wednesday, October 4
Dear Jay,

Wow, I can't believe it is Wednesday already. We are having a wonderful time. This place is so peaceful and serene, and we even learned how to meditate today. My mind is so clear and channeling such good energy. I've decided to grow hair under my arms, ditch the bra, and wear Birkenstocks—only joking, honey, although I do need a good shaving and a good bra. Later today, I will try rock climbing—how fun!

Love,

Bren

Dear Bren,

Do not rock climb, I repeat, *Do not rock climb!* You are needed at home. The kids still haven't mentioned you but *I* woke up screaming your name, among other things. To top things off, our girl is sick now, too. Same thing I have. Wonderful. Your schedule did come in handy because I had Dr. Leumas's cell number, pager number, and office number at my fingertips. I think these kids must have tapeworms. Seriously. I feed them dinner, and an hour later, I'm back in the kitchen making them something before bed. I feel like a short-order cook at a very unkempt diner. I try to go to the bathroom, and they are all over me. I can't get any time alone. Explain this, today I burst into tears for no reason, and I'm starting to feel fat. I know I'm rambling, but it is hard. Real hard. I think I need a new pair of shoes. Please have a safe trip home.

Jay

P.S. Did you happen to see today's episode of *Oprah*?

Thursday, October 5

Dear Jay,

Good morning, honey! I am looking out over the moonlit high desert sky. The moon is so bright, it is illuminating the canyon peaks. I can't wait to travel back here as a family. We are waiting on the shuttle to pick us up. I feel so relaxed, and I've had a wonderful week here with Ashley. We should be OM around 6:00 p.m., Louisiana time. Get it—OM, home. A little New Age humor for you, dear. I love you, and I love flying the friendly skies! Kiss the kids for me.

Bren

Dear Bren,

Six p.m.! That's another fourteen hours from now! OK, we'll be waiting. I forgot to tell you that Scott and I formed a small support group for husbands whose wives have left them with the children for five days and nights straight. There was lots of hugging and crying at the meeting. There was even a fetal-position moment, but we agreed not to share that with anyone. Oh, Miss Relaxed, wanted to let you know what I'm seeing out the window. I'm looking out over a mosquito-infested patio and a black Labrador retriever desperate for attention, but hey, glad you are loving the desert. I am hoping you left already and did not read this e-mail because it is not very nice, but I'm hitting send anyway. I'll try and hack in to your system and delete it from your inbox. But I'm still hitting send because it feels good.

Love,

Jay

P.S. Your meditation tips are *not* working.

Well, I arrived home to the children and a daddy running with arms wide open to Mommy. Picture a wheat field, wind blowing, and slow motion running. It feels good to be home, and it feels good to be needed. Namasté.

Chapter 26

Never Ever Say Never

If there were one piece of advice I could give to a couple that are planning on having kids, it would be to keep an open mind about how you will raise them. Before children, I found it very easy to judge others who had them, thinking I knew best. Over the past five years, I have eaten so many words that I can actually burp up whole phrases such as, "My kids will not sleep with me; they will be put to bed at 6:00 p.m. and will have to soothe themselves." Yeah, right. My children end up in my bed every night, leaving my husband and me on far sides of the universe. I do manage to stretch my leg way across the king-sized mattress, weaving through little legs, to put my toe on him. This is my way of saying goodnight and I love you. I've convinced him this is an old Native American gesture that means, "Despite the ponies among us, you remain a stallion." Poor thing believes me. Even the Navatoe tribe part.

A time ago, I also took a zero-tolerance stance on letting kids scream and make a fuss in a restaurant, or, even better, I thought their parents should not bring them at all. I came to this notion when I was a waitress in college. I despised waiting on customers with children. I thought kids were messy, disgusting little fried-chicken eaters who left a mound of crumbs under the high chair. The aftermath looked like a pack of beavers that chewed through a Sequoia tree had just left. Also, the parents thought they were so cute and laughed at every little gurgle, blabber, or scream. "Oh, we hope you don't mind … Little Timmy just threw the fifteenth spoon down on the floor.

Could you get us another one? Oh, and, waitress, could you make sure it is a teaspoon that is small, not an actual iced-tea spoon but also not a soup spoon, just a regular teaspoon." Coming right up. They even had the child perform for me like I really cared that Little Timmy could say bye-bye and water in three languages. To me, it sounded like he said "doo-doo," regardless of the word. How impressive, lady, your son just said poop in Swahili.

Well, the old I-told-you-so genie and the never-say-never police came to visit me once I had my own brood. Now I understand. I tip the waitress 800 percent, unless, of course, she brings me the wrong spoon. If we take the kids out, I make careful preparations to avoid public humiliation. We go when the restaurant opens, five o'clock sharp, hungry or not. We choose places that are frequented by families, but we still get the look when I ask for a high chair. I know what they are thinking, because I've been there, in the trenches, cleaning up after the miniature food tyrants. Now my son has been reincarnated as Little Timmy from twenty years ago. And I have become the doting-isn't-he-cute-when-he-does-that mother. "Oh, isn't he so precious when he dumps all of the Sweet-N-Low packets onto the floor?" Really, my son is like a homing pigeon with the artificial sweetener holder. He keeps going back to it and can find it wherever I hide it. He can eat through the pink paper like a termite on speed. But I can only see how beautiful the white powder looks next to his ocean blue eyes.

Another annoying behavior that parents have is trying to carry on a meaningful phone conversation with children screaming in the background. I remember avoiding phone calls from a friend years ago who was knee deep with three babies under the age of four. In the middle of a sentence, she would say, "I found the cutest shoes the other day at *shut up now!* They were chocolate brown suede with *what did I just say?* wedge heels." I remember telling her, "Please stop calling me until your children are over eighteen." I know that sounded rude, but because of the background noise, all she heard was the eighteen part. She thought I had found a pair of shoes on sale for that price.

Big revelation—I have become her, too! It's as though my children become possessed and get superhuman strength every time I am on the phone. They scream their loudest, jump their highest, fight like Mike Tyson, and hang on me like those gremlins from the movie. Maybe I should not feed them after midnight. The only time this behavior is acceptable is when I'm talking to another mom on the phone. *She* understands. It is like a support group and sometimes like a spectator sport. "Wow, Shelly, did you hear that echo? The baby just whacked his sister with a steel pipe, and she didn't even cry." But we also know the really bad screams or blood-curdling cries, the ones that make us hang up quickly. "Ooo, that one's gotta hurt, I'll call you later." The only time they seem to be quiet, perfect angels is when a telemarketer calls. Sometimes I'll have the baby answer when I see "out of area" on the caller ID. This has backfired on me, though. My son increased my credit line and bought me some life insurance just last week. He is a yes-man. Literally. Everything you ask him is "yes" but sounds like "yeah." I use it to my advantage at times. "Is Mommy pretty?" Yeah. "Can Mommy go two more weeks before getting her roots fixed?" Yeah. This reminds me when my daughter was one, she would hold up her index finger for almost everything. I used this to impress and amaze others. "Dear, how old are you?" Index finger up. "What is two minus one?" Index finger up. "What is eno spelled backwards?" Again, index up. "How many leaders are there in a dictatorship?" One! How brilliant one can look with a little manipulation and propaganda on the side.

Other things that have fallen into the "eating my words" category are home schooling (was I crazy!), never letting them watch television (violence, what violence?), and cloth diapers (rinse out *what?*). Yes, having children will completely throw your previous worldview and opinions into the big mixer of life. But don't worry. The outcome is a positive one—greater tolerance, fewer judgments, and love like no other.

Chapter 27

Candy Land

As Halloween approaches, a battle has begun, and the boxing gloves are off. My enemy is not the Boogeyman, the garden-variety werewolf, or Wal-Mart on a Saturday. My enemy is all powerful, sneaky, slippery, and sticky and has infiltrated my home. My enemy is candy. Yes, candy, and I will eat it, I mean, defeat it, one Tootsie Roll at a time. It is everywhere and is in the forefront of my children's minds. It is all they want and all they need to survive.

As I watch their big eyes light up at the sight of a lollipop or cotton candy, I am reminded of a research study I learned about in college. Mice were given a choice of liquid sugar or food, ratatouille, I think. Of course, they ate themselves into oblivion with the sugar water and developed adult-onset type 2 mouse diabetes. The mice also became obese, moody, and tired. A few of the mice, the smart ones from the lab, recognized the problem and started using a sugar substitute. *Nutria*-Sweet rings a bell. Or was that Saccarat? They bought high-tech hamster wheels to work out on, used them only once, and then began to hang their little mouse clothes on them. My kids will become those mice if I let them. My son is already crawling into spaces that don't seem humanly possible, and my daughter has developed a fear of cats for some reason.

Who can blame them? Candy is readily available and at their fingertips. Grocery stores, drugstores, and convenience stores have colorful candy displays strategically positioned at eye level—the children's eye level. My children take advantage of long grocery lines and decide to barter for candy. My daughter would give up her brother for a pack of SweetTarts and a stick of gum. I usually give in and pick the lesser evil, the candy with the peanuts. At least I know they will be getting a little protein. Once my son whittles the chocolate away, I am left with freshly chewed-up nuts spit right into my hand. Moms hold the grossest things!

The problem with Halloween is that candy possession starts about two weeks before the actual night of trick-or-treating. How can it be that my kids already have a jack-o'-lantern filled with candy, and October 31 is not even here yet? Sources of candy include any birthday party in the month of October, school parties, gymnastics class, the bank drive-thru, and grandmothers. All of this exposure to sugar builds up their immunity and tolerance so that on Halloween night, they consume much more than the average child from, say, 1950.

Times may have changed, but costumes haven't. When I was seven years old, I decided to be Snow White for Halloween. I couldn't wait for the evening to roll around so that I could put on my beautiful costume and Snow White mask. No one would ever know that I was a toothless wonder underneath it all. Twirling in the beautiful dress, I distinctly remember the anticipation I felt as I awaited my complete transformation into the Disney Princess. As my mom slipped the plastic mask over my little blond noggin, the tiny elastic strap snapped. Darn it! For a quick repair, I hummed for my cartoon bluebirds to fly in, but they didn't show up. I think they were busy with Cinderella that night. Even without the mask, at least I could look forward to trick-or-treating. By the end of the night, I had one bag full of goodies and I was as happy as a fairy tale character could be. The amount of candy I received was about 20 percent of what my children get these days.

My candy battle continues, and I am starting to think I will not be the victor. You see, just this week, I caught my son sitting in the middle of his room, jack-o'-lantern dumped out, and his loot spread evenly on the floor. His mouth was filled with candy, and he looked and talked like Don Corleone from *The Godfather*. Strangely, he was wearing a Lifesavers ring on his pinky finger and smoking a candy cigarette. He kissed me on both cheeks and smiled, but I sensed trouble was around the corner. That night, I found a rocking horse's head in my bed. I knew then to back off the jack-o'-lantern, or else.

Chapter 28

Got Prozac?

Whew, what a challenging week this has been. It has been one of those weeks when I feel like a dog chasing her tail. It so happens that I have qualified for other titles involving female canines, so my husband says. The week was not anything unusual other than Halloween trick-or-treating and, oh, some mild bloating. It was just a week when the planets aligned themselves in a way that did not match my galaxy. Speaking of galaxies, the bite-size Milky Way bars that I ate every day didn't agree with me either, but that didn't stop me. The last seven days brought heavy traffic around every turn, kids throwing up in the car, a dishwasher needing repair, mosquito infestations, nightmares of West Nile taking me and leaving my children motherless, and my old favorite tried and true feeling of having a "fat" week.

This all leads to less quality family time and absolutely no time with my husband. I've compared him to the meteorologist back in the studio on the Weather Channel during a major hurricane—calm, sitting with a warm cup of coffee at his fingertips and in a controlled environment. I, on the other hand, am the rookie meteorologist reporting from the eye of the storm, barely clinging to a light pole with debris swirling around her. The studio guy has the nerve to say, "Sorry, we can't hear you, Susie. Let's go now to Jim who is in Napa Valley covering the annual wine-tasting festival. What a beautiful day it is there, eh, Jim?" Meanwhile, Susie has let go of the light pole and is sailing through the air holding on to a manhole cover, but she is still warm and dry thanks to her trusty, royal blue North Face parka.

So during crazy, busy times, my husband starts to miss me. I must admit, I am very "missable." He will bring this to my attention before I ever realize that I haven't had a nonfragmented conversation with him or a real kiss for days. Before he leaves in the morning, I give him one of those side-swipe kisses accompanied with a faint, trailing "love you." He gingerly reminds me that we haven't had so much as a full hug the entire week. Then, I must remind him that I have touched him plenty this week. However, it occurred in the middle of the night. He just doesn't realize it. You see, I am an expert with a maneuver I'll call the Snore Stopper. It is a brisk flick of the lower leg, just from the knee down, but with power so great, I may have to license it. I liken it to the one-inch punch that was Bruce Lee's trademark. It is lightning fast, and he doesn't even know what hit him. The snoring stops immediately, and he just turns over. I imagine it is difficult to snore and moan at the same time. Mission accomplished.

Fortunately, my husband is a very patient man. He is calm, level-headed, and puts up with fourteen days a month of PMS. For me, PMS wears many hats. It is convenient and works well in most situations. It is an acronym for the obvious and the not-so-obvious. Let's just label it "Plenty of Mood Swings." For example, every night after 5:00 p.m., I morph into the ghost of Joan Crawford. I don't know what it is, but I was so nice in the morning after my coffee. After dark, I have zero tolerance for whining, messes, homework, and wire hangers. I think my daughter is already working on a book about me, and I've even found a rough draft of the manuscript in her book sack. Between my crankiness and lack of cooking abilities, a good working title would be *Chicken Soup for the Other Families of the World, Except Mine* or maybe *War and Peas*. Yes, I like that one better.

My husband and I have surrendered to the fact that our marriage has evolved and can now be described as "teamwork" since our children arrived. We love each other on a deeper level, and we both have great respect for the roles we each have in the family. Cue up an "aww." There are times (nightly) that I bring to his attention how difficult my role is. Over and over. He is a patient man.

Language also changes after kids. For example, we no longer refer to each other by our respective names, Brenna and Jay. We are now "Mommy" and "Daddy," even when the kids aren't around. When my kids are asking about playing ball outside, I'll say, "Daddy, what do think? Can you go out with them for a few minutes? Yeah! Thanks, Daddy." This is just plain weird. I even refer to myself in third person when addressing the kids or him. "Mommy is very tired. Mommy needs a few minutes to take a shower without kids banging on the door." "Did you hear Mommy?" "Mommy is about to snap!" I've even called the hair salon once and said, "Mommy needs a highlight and a cut." "Excuse me?" comes from the other end of the line, and I quickly say, "*Monday*, I need a highlight and a cut."

Other words such as stomach, bruise, and bathroom are replaced with tummy, boo-boo, and potty. When my kids aren't with me, I sometimes forget to switch languages and will ask the hostess of a very nice restaurant where the potty is or tell the doctor I've been having tummy aches. I guess I'm not the only one who does this, because sometimes, the doctor will offer *me* a sucker—he must have kids, too.

Chapter 29

The Doctor's Office

It seems as though I've committed a crime, a revolting act that warrants punishment from my fellow man. The crime, you wonder? I brought my two-year-old son with me for my annual thyroid check up. As soon as we walked in, I could read the look on the faces of the office personnel and the patients in the lobby. I thought I heard the snowy egret in the framed Audubon print on the wall cautiously caw—a fight or flight kind of thing.

I feel like I am a proficient mind reader, and on that day in the doctor's office, many messages were coming my way. When I signed in, holding my snorting little toddler on my hip, the receptionist grinned but not in a nice way. More in the why-did-you-bring-that-thing-in-here way. She was not up for small talk, only co-pays. She obviously does not have children. But maybe she does.

I scanned the lobby for a quiet corner for us to sit down. I also scanned the floor with my portable ultraviolet bacteria detector, and after reviewing the slides on my nifty key-chain microscope, I found only a few strains of unharmful streptococcus. Nothing a wet wipe couldn't kill.

I spotted a sweet-looking little old lady and decided to sit next to her. I thought she would be very engaging and would want to discuss her grandchildren with me. Certainly *she* wouldn't mind him crawling around. I expected the usual "How old is he?" and the "What is his name?" questions, but it didn't quite go that way. She glanced over at me and then let out a muffled cough, acting as though she needed water. She casually meandered to the coffee table, picked up a copy of *Motorcycling Enthusiast*, and then sat as far away from us as possible.

I thought for a minute that my child must have turned red, grown horns, and stuck out a forked tongue. I mean, really, he is a human. I've seen the DNA report myself. He will not bite (usually) and is very cute.

Once ostracized, we settled into our space, and that is when I discovered the fear of all mothers—a doctor's office toy box! It was filled with cruddy Legos, a doll missing an eye, and the shell of a *Highlights* magazine. By the looks of it, it was obviously meant to discourage parents from bringing their children here. I was surprised we didn't find a set of Ginsu knives or a lead-making kit inside. The *Highlights* magazine alone shorted out my bacteria detector. Well, so much for reading the latest issue of *Endocrinology Today*—I would have to watch him carefully and prepare for the slow-motion tackle if he decided to taste one of the crusty pieces.

We were evading the lobby radar and all was well, until he found a lone drumstick at the bottom of the toy box. He looked at me excitedly with his big blue eyes, knowing he had found something special. Then, in sync to the beat of the drum and with perfect cadence, he shouted, "Mom-my, me poo-poo, yeah!" Although the situation called for mild embarrassment, I didn't see it that way. I recognized his musical prowess and was quite proud—it is in his genes from his daddy's side, you know. I knew the lobby people were thinking, "Yeah, it's in his jeans, all right!"

Because I am kind to others, I took him outside to change the diaper. I had to lay him in my trunk with his little white hiney shining for all passersby. We returned to the lobby just in time for my name to be called. "Mrs. Bar-zen-a-witch." I was in no mood to correct her, so off we trotted through the door.

As soon as my son saw the nurse's uniform, he lost it. He started screaming, *"No shot! No shot! Noooo shot!"* Oh boy, he was having a flashback from the flu-vaccine experience a few weeks ago. From that point on, it was all a blur. He was offered suckers, crackers, a reindeer ink-pen, blood-pressure cuffs, and, I think at one point, a cigarette. The doctor even advised it. Nothing worked to calm or distract him, so my appointment was cut short. Again, all eyes were on me as I was forced to reschedule with the lovely receptionist that greeted us earlier.

So, off we went, my little guy and me for the long drive back home and feeling glad to have left the no-kid zone. As I pulled out of the parking lot, I saw a flash of something white in my rearview mirror. Gee, what was that? A flyer? A bird? A plane? Oh my gosh, the dirty diaper! Great, they can now add "litterbug" to my medical chart along with the title of "Woman with Screaming Child."

Chapter 30

A Day in the Life

These days, it is amazing what is considered news, especially "breaking news." The mundane has become sensational, and the horrific has become routine and numbing. Having said that, I wonder if a day in my life would ever be considered newsworthy or interesting to others. Perhaps it could be the premise for a new reality TV show? I'll give it a try and share my itinerary from last Tuesday.

3:00 a.m.: My son staggers into my room asking for wa-wa and grits. I give him a sip of water and tell him the grits will have to wait until the morning. There is no going back to his room, so I let him nuzzle up to me. His hair smells good.

3:12 a.m.: Almost back asleep, I am awakened by the sound of the space shuttle re-entering the atmosphere. Oh wait, that was just a grunt and a snort from my husband. I poise myself for a field-goal-type kick in his direction, but he stops making noises just in time.

4:57 a.m.: Nature calls. Really. I think there is a large predatory bird just outside my window stalking the neighbor's miniature dachshund. I hear growling, hissing, cawing, and screeching. My mind gets the best of me, and I begin to second guess the bird idea. I begin to wonder if there is a boa constrictor on the loose. Then my mind starts to focus on the hissing, and I begin to convince myself that there is a gas leak outside. Oh boy, could it be? The house could blow at any minute. It will start a chain reaction in the neighborhood. Mayhem! Chaos! Confusion! I really need to take swift action and sound the neighborhood warning siren. Sadly, we don't have one, and after all, I am really, really tired. I'll just lie here a few minutes.

5:00 a.m.: Oops, I dozed off. Oh good, no explosion! I'll just mark the hissing up to a mysterious noise not otherwise specified.

5:05 a.m.: I decide to get up and make coffee. I welcome the quiet darkness in my home. I check e-mail and visit weather.com. Another pretty day in the forecast. I think I will try to meditate. Not levitate or anything, just empty my mind and set my intentions for the day. I curl up in my favorite chair, light a candle that smells like almond biscotti, and start to slow my breathing. Yum, almond biscotti with some hazelnut gelato on the side. Clear your mind, Brenna. Focus. Breathe.

5:06 a.m.: While meditating, I hear the sound of my stomach growling. I'm starving, but, hey, didn't Gandhi go on a hunger strike? A little hunger and sacrifice never hurt anyone. Focus. Breathe. Chant. Om. Om. "Home, home on the range, where the deer and the antelope play …" Focus, brain! Clear your mind, grasshopper. Stop singing! "Singing in the rain …" There you go again. You have officially failed at meditating.

5:15 a.m.: Nature calls again, and I answer. Wow, how nice it is to have privacy in the bathroom for a change. I flip through a few catalogs and study the dirt that has collected on my baseboards. I'll put that on my to-do list for sure.

5:30 to 6:00 a.m.: I start a load of clothes, feed the dog, empty the garbage can, and take my thyroid medication. I catch a glimpse of myself in the mirror. Forty is approaching quickly, and I wonder if Sam's Wholesale sells under-eye concealer in bulk. I'll buy a vat if they have it.

6:00 a.m.: Time to wake my daughter for school. I never look forward to this. I go into her room, and I open the blinds ever so slightly. In my sweetest tone of voice: "Honey, time to wake uuuup. It is going to be a beautiful day, sweetie." No response. I guess she can sleep for a few more minutes.

6:05 a.m.: "Baby, time to get up. Mommy let you sleep a little longer, so please rise and shine."

She says, "But I don't want to go to school. I'm tired. I'm cold. I want to go back to sleep!" Lucky for her, the baby has awakened and wants his grits now. Right now. He wants to pour the grits in the bowl, mix in the water, and push the buttons on the microwave. "Me do, me do!" he demands. Half the grits get spilled on the counter, and I am holding back my frustration. I mean, heck, I just meditated twenty minutes ago. The grits are ready, but they have to cool off. This can take forever, just as it does with other heat-retaining foods like macaroni and cheese and mashed potatoes. Lava cools faster than these foods.

6:07 a.m.: With a loud tone of voice I say, "Get up now! If we get another tardy, Mommy is going to jail for contributing to the truancy of a minor."

She casually says, "What does contributing mean?"

"It means adding to," I say.

"Like two plus two?" she replies.

"No, honey, I'll explain it when we have more time."

6:08 a.m.: "How many times do I have to say get out of bed? I think I'll make an appointment with an ear doctor, because you obviously have a hearing problem!" I threaten.

"What does obviously mean?" she says.

Big sigh.

6:08 to 7:30 a.m.: She is finally up. I guess the idle threats and the dose of dysfunction worked. I'll summarize this window of time as a race against the clock. It is kind of like when someone wins a shopping spree and they have only three minutes to fill their grocery cart with whatever they can grab. Now, visualize a whirlwind of overnight diapers full and flying, Pop-Tarts crumbling, toothpaste on chins, and matted hair. This scene is followed by turning the car on two wheels around corners, accelerating through yellow lights while the kids endure mild g-forces, and sliding stunt-driver style into the church parking lot. Yes, we made it! Amen. I also think the magnetic police light and combination siren I bought was very helpful.

8:00 a.m. to 12:00 p.m.: We are back at home, and this block of time mostly involves cleaning up from the aftermath of the morning. Fortunately, I do not feel rushed, and I can take my time picking up toys, doing dishes, and making beds. I do have a small hang-up when it comes to dolls. For some reason, I have to make sure their heads are facing forward and all of the plastic limbs are aligned correctly. I like to think it is because I am a physical therapist and it makes sense orthopedically. However, they are just dolls. I also have to keep them out of a toy box in the fresh air. Yes, I know I have a problem. Maybe I can start taking PhenoBarbie-tol for it.

12:00 to 2:00 p.m.: I repeat the above routine except for the dolls, plus I have to put the cushions back on the sofa, again. My son takes the cushions off of the sofa about a hundred times a day. My daughter did the same thing when she was two. There must be a DNA mutation in our family that causes pillow disarrangement.

2:00 p.m.: I leave home and head to the carpool line. No police light necessary. The baby falls asleep on the way there, and I am grateful for another brief moment of silence.

2:35 p.m.: I see my daughter getting her book sack and waiting for my car to pull up under the breezeway. She is really starting to get tall. I realize how much I missed her today. On the way home, I ask her how her day was, and she responds, "Good."

"Did you fall asleep during naptime?" I ask.

"No," she says.

"What did they serve in the cafeteria today?" I ask her.

"I don't remember, but, Mommy, did you know that Jupiter has a huge storm on it, and the storm itself is bigger than Earth?" she says.

"That is fascinating, honey."

2:35 to 4:00 p.m.: My son naps during this time, and I bribe my daughter with gum so she will keep quiet and let him sleep. When we arrive home, I catch a few minutes of *Oprah*, and we start homework. There is one worksheet that has confused me, so I have to call her teacher. How embarrassing, but she assures me that grown-ups have trouble with kindergarten homework all of the time. Sure.

4:00 p.m.: My son wakes up, and my daughter immediately asks for the chewing gum. Well, my son overhears this and screams for a piece, too. As he is only two and a half years old, I am not comfortable with him chewing gum, but I let him have it anyway. I think gum chewing should be added to the developmental milestones. Hold head up, sit up independently, crawl, walk, and chew gum without swallowing. I remind him that he must spit it out and he cannot swallow it. Well, so much for that. He has managed to swallow the equivalent of twenty pieces in his lifetime so far. I remember hearing when I was small that it takes four years to digest one piece of gum. So, if my math serves me right, when he is eighty years old and goes in for a colonoscopy, the doctor may mistake the wad of Juicy Fruit for a large, benign polyp.

4:15 to 6:00 p.m.: I let them play outside while I sort the mail and read the paper. I pull a few weeds in the flowerbed and kill a few wasps with the nineteen-and-a-half-foot spray (dollar-store special). I also think about what we will have for supper. Drive-thru or delivery, that is the question.

6:00 to 7:00 p.m.: First there is bathtime, followed by dinner. We like to keep the television off during this time. My husband and I talk about our day, and we enjoy our family time.

7:00 p.m.: American Idol starts, and we wonder how bad the auditions will be this week. We love this show and have become quite proficient in recognizing pitch. Even my kids agree with Simon most of the time. The kids want cereal, and they eat again.

8:00 p.m.: Time for bed and books.

8:20 p.m.: Lights out.

8:25 p.m.: My son starts to whine for a snack. I comfort him and hope he will fall asleep fast.
8:30 to midnight: I actually get three and a half hours of uninterrupted sleep. Yippee!

So it goes, my own reality show. What shall I call it? *Survivor*? *The Surreal Life*? *The Amazing Race*? I've got it! How about *Are You Smarter than a Kindergartner?* Sometimes, not.

Chapter 31

Midlife Celebration

The word going around is that forty is the new twenty. I think this is supposed to be encouraging for women who may be fretting the forty-year milestone. For me, I like the idea of turning forty. I like the way *forty* rolls off of my tongue. *Thirty* is challenging to perfect diction. The slight lisp I had in second grade attempts to sneak back in, or out I should say, when I use any word beginning with *th*. My tongue wants to go beyond my front teeth. Saying forty is easy. My tongue behaves and remains in its confined space. So, with my fortieth birthday just around the corner, I find myself wiser, more relaxed, and finally comfortable in my skin (albeit a little stretchier and pleated). Plus, I don't *feel* forty, whatever that is supposed to feel like. I've thought, with my son turning three in a few weeks, is three the new one? With so many twenty-year-olds suntanning year round, they don't know it, but they are the new eighty.

I have started to become more introspective. Soulfully inquisitive. So, what have I learned over these almost-forty years? Being a professed, maniacal list-maker, I cannot resist the occasion to start composing and numbering, so here it goes.

1. Children will unequivocally, irreversibly, and undeniably rock your world.
2. If a video camera were to be used in my bedroom, its strict purpose would be to capture my husband snoring and prove to him that he is louder than an F-5 tornado.

3. Never clean lint out of the dryer screen with wet fingertips.
4. If a friend or an acquaintance calls and uses ambiguous phrases such as "I have this really great opportunity I would like to talk to you about" or "I wanted to let you in on this product that Oprah is about to endorse," then know that you will be the bottom rung of a marketing pyramid ladder.
5. Be alert. Lord knows this world could use more lerts. (I do not take credit for this one; I read it in *Reader's Digest* and loved it.)
6. Functional families just don't exist, and the word *dysfunctional* is now an endearing term, and quite frankly, part of normal conversation. "You think that's dysfunctional, you should hear about my Aunt Irma who, by the way, we now call Uncle Earl."
7. The world will end if I do not check e-mail twenty times a day and visit weather.com at least five times a day.
8. Seek inner peas. Yes, I meant to say peas. I found a molded crop of them that my son buried between the sofa cushions. They were from a dinner I made last February. Capital-G Gross.
9. *To Kill a Mockingbird* continues to be the best book I've ever read, and I read a lot.
10. I've stopped watching the news. It is overstimulating, depressing, and numbing. If there is something I really need to know, I'm confident I will hear about it in town.
11. I know how many carbohydrate grams there are in all foods including rutabagas.
12. I realize that Mary Ann from *Gilligan's Island* is really the one I would like to be. Make that Mrs. Howell with Ginger's body and Mary Ann's values.
13. I cannot text message or e-mail anyone without using proper punctuation. It just doesn't feel right.
14. Nine thirty p.m. is way too late for anything.
15. All women are beautiful, powerful, and universally connected. I embrace this. Together we can change the world.
16. What you resist, persists.
17. Being needed and being loved by my husband and babies is all I will ever need, hands down.
18. I enjoy going to children's birthday parties so I can eat the cake.
19. I am not comfortable being at a red light next to someone I know. Fiddling with the radio can only get you so far. Pretending to turn and talk to your children works better.
20. I have developed a personal policy. When people know you have a policy, they are more apt to take no for an answer. For example,

"Sorry, but it is my policy to never lend money to friends or family." Enough said. "I wish I could listen to your sales pitch with interest, but I have a policy to never purchase or donate anything over the telephone." Again, no rebuttal necessary. "Thanks for considering me, but I have a policy for not getting involved in multilevel marketing" (see number four above).

21. I've learned that I can stop my lists on an odd number and not lose sleep over it.

Well, I'll admit that was quite therapeutic. I'll keep adding entries to my list and report back to you occasionally. I'm sure when I'm fifty, I'll have a new list that starts with "1. You ain't seen nothing yet!"

Chapter 32

The First Step Is Admitting You Have a Problem

Hello, my name is Brenna, I am a Fox News addict, and this is my story. I can proudly say that I'm going on four months now without watching the news on television or the Internet. My soul, my inner being and presence pulled an intervention on me. You see, I was losing myself in a pool of negativity, and I was caught in the grips of an ostensible Fair and Balanced newscast. The problem was that my psyche was getting *fairly unbalanced.*

My daily fix of bad news brought with it many side effects. For one, I was certain that a mild sniffle and cough was the avian flu or a superbacteria resistant to all antibiotics. I even had the family enrolled in an advanced swim class and helicopter-basket rescue training just in case we were caught in a local flash flood. The news provided me with endless worry about loose pythons, toxic mold, and identity theft. My husband also became an unknowing suspect in the Anna Nicole Smith paternity suit. That baby does favor him—bald, cute, and gassy.

Since turning off the news completely, I must say I feel more relaxed and more at peace with the world. I am not burying my head in the sand or being passive, I have simply made a choice not to force feed myself bad news and then have to digest every kidnapping, homicide, genocide, police chase, embarrassing political scandal, terrorist threat, and drug-trafficking story in

America and abroad. You see, images and tragic stories do not bounce off of me; they become rooted in my thoughts. We are an empathetic, loving, and rational species, so how could hearing a steady stream of bad news not eat away at our spirits, crumb by crumb?

I am not sure I would have come to this decision if I didn't have children. When the news is on in the house, they hear it too. Invariably, questions are asked. As you know, some information is not appropriate for little ears (or big ears for that matter). To me, modern newscasts are an experiment in overstimulation and desensitization. My head would be knotted and my eyes crossed after trying to keep up with a newscast. There were questionable "breaking" news flashes accompanied by tickers on the bottom of the screen. All of this while a perky anchorwoman recited news copy to dramatic music. It was a feeling similar to trying to sneeze, pee, and scratch at the same time. One has to win over the other, but they all have your attention. If you've ever birthed babies or reached midlife, then you know that sneezing and peeing become one act altogether. Well, that Depends …

My opinion is that if just half of our population turned off the television, then together, our collective thought patterns could be filled with pleasant feelings and goodwill. A friend of mine told me she visited Croatia this summer, and it was a friendly, lively place where neighbors gathered and people sat around eating and having conversation. It is tradition and a very important ritual for them as a community. In America, we think we do not have the time to visit or share stories or just say hello for five minutes. We could and we should. I say, let us stop, shake hands, give someone a hug, or call someone instead of e-mailing, by gosh. Use your house phone if you still have one. I recently read about a management course that was called, "Developing Interpersonal Communication Skills in the Workplace." Ironically, it was offered as an online course only! Amazing.

Eventually, my goal is to become unplugged completely. I am the only one in my family who could do without the television. My daughter loves to watch *Hannah Montana* on the Disney channel, and my son loves *Diego*. My husband watches the Tennis Channel and then all the channels for ten seconds each before he starts over from the beginning. It has affected his hearing but only while the television is on. Strange, huh?

I must say that it is tempting to watch the news when it is on at a restaurant or at someone's home, but in my house, I practice the twelve steps of news recovery. That is to say, the distance from my recliner to the off button on the television—twelve steps exactly.

Chapter 33

The Big One

This week I reached my forty-year-old milestone. I'm not sure if milestones still apply to adults, but I thought I could start a new trend of recognizing grown-up accomplishments. I've kept track of when my children first sat up, walked, and spoke, so why not record events that mark turning points in my life? I wonder if there is a book big enough.

My daughter, being the first born, has a baby book that is meticulously charted and time-stamped with her milestones, vaccination records, first-tooth eruption, baby-shower gift list, my pregnancy test stick, first ultrasound pictures, birth announcement, and a list of all the visitors who came to see her at the hospital. The organization and preciseness of the entries rival a flight log from a NASA space-shuttle mission. First burp, check. Incoming gas bubble, check. Mommy's weight after delivery—data lost.

When my son came along, I knew I would be just as conscientious about filling out his baby book. Well, I wrote in his name and weight measurements, I threw in the hospital birth picture where he resembled a newborn squirrel, and I left him a sealed letter to be opened when he turns eighteen years old. The letter reads,

> Dear Son,
> You were such a precious and cuddly child, I could not bear to put you down. I held you all day long and, contrary to

what it may seem, I only have two arms. Between nursing you, changing your diaper, and carrying you, I just didn't have the extra time to sit and write. Please know that all of your milestones are forever etched in my memory. Moms have an uncanny ability to remember minute details about their children. It is instinctive and should never be questioned. Know that I treasure your first word at three months old, your first laugh, which occurred in the womb during the first cell division, and when you took those shaky first steps at age fourteen. You are the best!

I love you,

Mom

I'm still wondering how to explain the scarce inventory of three photographs of him as a baby (ages one, two, and three), while his sister has an expandable portfolio that could be presented to the Ford Modeling Agency.

All right, enough about those children. I have reached several major adult milestones such as marriage, motherhood, investments, mortgages, and picket fences. While they are important and wonderful accomplishments, they are far from unusual. I like the unusual. So, I will attempt to create an out-of-the-ordinary milestone checklist for myself. I will describe a few little quirks and habits that have manifested in my life at forty.

1. The Tissue Issue—I spend at least seven minutes of precious grocery-shopping time selecting the décor of a Kleenex box. Strictly no florals unless it is a single zinnia or sunflower. And that is only during the spring or summer months. Geometric patterns are also avoided—too much of a 1980s flare. I prefer oval boxes but will settle for a traditional shape if necessary. Definitely no mauve, blue, or pink tissue. Those scream, "nursing home." The box must have a contemporary theme but still be versatile in each room of the house. Gesundheit.
2. A Bedtime Lullaby—join me in singing, "Tinkle, tinkle little star, it's 2:00 a.m., and the toilet's not far. Up above the bathroom light, I see a mosquito in the night (and I can't sleep now 'cause it's going to bite!). Tingle, tingle itchy sore, gee look at the clock, it's almost four!"
3. Introducing Oscar winner, Meryl *Sleep*—my uncanny ability to deliver an Academy Award–winning performance of perfect stillness. With the focus and will of a Tibetan monk, I am able to slow down

my heart rate, breathing, and muscle activity so that I appear to be in a deep state of sleep in order to avoid a frisky husband. *Note:* Coffee will be strategically spilled on this sentence prior to his reading of my book.

4. InDISHision—trying to decide if I should let my husband load the dishwasher, knowing all the while I will have to rearrange it anyway.
5. Not Quilty—I have tortured myself with the purchase of a duvet cover for my bed. I long for a simple quilt or bedspread. I've decided that anything with a French name proves to be difficult in one way or another. Sheer pronunciation of *duvet* is a challenge. I thought it rhymed with *muffet* until my friend Marguerite politely told me otherwise. The goose-down comforter inside of the duvet bunches at my feet and is difficult to straighten. No wonder I cannot sleep. Will I recover?
6. The Green Tile—I have developed a habit of counting ceiling tiles while at the doctor's office. When I'm waiting in the examination room, I start counting to pass the time. I always recheck my calculations if time permits. Exam room three of my internist's office has forty-four ceiling tiles to be exact. Room eight of my gynecologist's office has thirteen and a half tiles, and this odd number bothers me, of course. Add in the stirrups, and it is one stressful visit.

I dare not venture any further for risk of being considered officially nuts. And, if the men in white coats come to get me, I'll bet they will be driving (again, join me in singing) "a knick, knack paddy wagon …"

Chapter 34

On the Road Again

I've always wanted a second home. Maybe in the mountains or by the ocean or even a horse ranch in Montana. Well, two kids later, I now realize that I got my wish, though not exactly the way I'd dreamed it. My second home is made of black steel, glass, plastic, and rubber. It is my car. I spend more time in it than I would like. If my life were a movie, the theme song would be Johnny Cash's "I've Been Everywhere."

My car does have some properties of a real home. It comes complete with a kitchen, where we eat breakfast and afternoon snacks, a garbage disposal (on the seat, under the seat, and in all crevices), a bathroom (wet diapers tossed here and there), a living room (DVD player, CD player), a play room (balls, toys, blocks, books, markers, crayons), and an office (cell phone, planner, purse, calendar) on the front seat. We also have an exercise room. Unfortunately, only my right arm gets a workout. It is now about two inches longer than the left due to all the repetitive reaching to the backseat. Even though I am only five foot two, I could easily dunk a basketball with my right arm.

Let's not forget the garage—my trunk. It houses a golf umbrella, two strollers, an emergency kit, more diapers, a change of clothes for the entire family in case we are stranded in a snow storm or something, a bag of donated items for Goodwill, a tool box, jumper cables, and a grocery organizer.

My car seems to be just another source of stress for me. I rush to get out of the house, leaving behind dirty dishes in the sink, clothes on the floor, beds unmade, soggy cereal on the table, and toilets unflushed only to get into my car and experience yet another mess. I've bought trash receptacles, over-the-seat organizers, upholstery protectors, and cord wraps for cell-phone chargers, but to no avail. Kids are the problem. They are natural pack rats. You would think mine grew up in the Depression era, because they horde everything. My car was spotless before the little crumb crunchers came into my life. Now, I've even had to tint my windows so the clutter can be obscured from plain view.

The list of things in my car that are unnecessary for basic travel is endless. We just can't seem to leave the house without my daughter bringing two purses, a pink scarf, bubblegum lip gloss, a writing tablet, and a princess pen. My son has to bring his Buzz Lightyear doll, a flashlight, his new big-boy Spider-Man underwear, and a box of raisins. It would be just fine if all of the stuff made it back into the house the same day, but of course, it doesn't. It just keeps piling up and piling up.

Just leaving the house is a challenge. I don't know what takes so long to get out the door. I'm sure that astronauts have a smaller checklist than mine before takeoff. The same goes for getting *out* of the car. The kids meander and seem to move in slow motion. I am constantly nagging them to "Come on, hurry up, get out!" I wonder sometimes what I sound like to other people in the parking lot. Especially when I have to wrestle my three-year-old into his car seat with him kicking and screaming loudly … very loudly. He always manages to scream, "No, Stop!" when he doesn't want to get buckled up. I sometimes daydream about the shopping-center surveillance camera capturing the moment and Fox News picking up the so-called "breaking news" story. "We have breaking news. We've obtained exclusive video of a woman in Louisiana forcing her child into the car. Look closely and you can see the little boy attempting to get away from her grasp. What a scene, ladies and gentleman, turn away if you must, because the next part is disturbing. She is bending over, and her low-waisted jeans are revealing what appears to be granny underwear. This lady really has problems. What is she doing now? My goodness, she is scrubbing his little hands with some sort of foamy cloth. Bill, could you zoom in on that please? Yes, it is an antibacterial wipe, and she is aggressively scrubbing his little hands while he cries. Someone needs to stop this woman!" Fortunately, I snap out of my mental movie and realize that could never happen. I mean, granny underwear is for nighttime only.

Aside from all the complaining, I do have enjoyable moments in my car. I love the quiet time I get when I am in the afternoon carpool line. It seems to be the only time of day where I am still for fifteen minutes or so. My son falls asleep every day around carpool time, so I truly have peace and quiet. I read the paper, file my nails, or just close my eyes for a few minutes. I'll sometimes get in line thirty minutes ahead of time so I can catch a power nap. With that said, I guess the latest addition to my second home—my car—would be a meditation room. Ah, nice.

Chapter 35

The Christmas Play

I was feeling a bit Scroogey until last Wednesday at 12:30 p.m. I attended my daughter's kindergarten Christmas play, and I was changed in an instant. The stay-at-home mom of Christmas past was, for once, in the present. The play was a reenactment of the Nativity, and the children were all dressed in costumes to play their parts—the wise men, shepherds, stable animals, inn keepers, angels, the star of Bethlehem, and, of course, Mary and Joseph. They were all so perfect and were joyous in their participation. I was moved. Literally. I changed spots countless times so I could get the perfect video angle of my daughter's performance. I did not want to miss this event that will forever live on a digital tape and will probably not be seen until the year 2525 when archeologists find it in a dig. They may need a little Christmas spirit in the future, who knows?

The same morning of the play, I was complaining to myself about the holiday season. Christmas was supposed to be a wonderful time of year with jingle bells ringing, hot-chocolate sipping, and mistletoe above us. Instead, it has become cell phones ringing, chocolate any way I can get it, and forget the mistletoe altogether—it is poisonous and promotes a level of intimacy that I just do not have time for.

Every year around this time, I get fed up with all the hustle and bustle surrounding Christmas. I want it to be a special time for my children, and I do my best to make it about them, not about how frazzled Mommy is. Why does this beautiful season have to be stressful? I would love for my family to travel in a time machine back to a year when life was simple and Christmas was a celebration of spirituality, togetherness, and family. No television, computers, inflatable Santas, or crowded malls. My children would be happy with one gift each—a baby doll for my daughter and a stick horse for my son. One can dream, eh?

However, this is a time of excess. I think, as a society, we have too much, but we still want more. More. More. And more. We bombard our children with so many gifts, I have to wonder what good it does. The giving seems to be year round. I have to sort through the toys and games they already possess to make room for the new stuff that Santa will bring. I am left shaking my head and thinking, "How do I teach my kids the value of money, patience, and earning things?" All of this deep thinking makes me very cranky.

Aside from the gift giving, there is the Christmas-card photograph that can make any mom snap—I'm not talking shutter speed here. This year I was smart and had a professional take the picture. This way, I knew the kids would not be traumatized by me yelling at them to look at me, be still, and smile while I took their picture. Last Christmas, I was lucky to get one decent snapshot of the kids in their Christmas attire, looking peaceful and sweet. Thank goodness for digital-photography editing—I was able to shade in the tears and crop the old bunny-ears trick my daughter pulled behind my son's head.

The Christmas season also leaves me feeling inadequate in certain areas. For one, all the catalogs in the mail show decorated home interiors with fancy mantels, garland everywhere, sparkling place settings, and candelabras defining the dining table. I'll be lucky to match my Dixie paper plates with a seasonal paper towel. Maybe this year I'll go all out and get the Chinet brand.

Just the other day, I even saw a few cars decorated for Christmas. A wreath was neatly attached to the grill with a brilliant red bow adorning it. This must help in traffic. I mean, who could have road rage against the nice people who took the time to decorate their car, for goodness sakes?

Meanwhile, back at the auditorium, I was suddenly brought back into the moment as my little girl stood up to speak her part in the play. I gleamed with pride as she said her lines perfectly. I felt my seasonal moodiness dissolving in an instant. That day, I was reminded of Robert Fulghum's book *All I Really Need to Know I Learned in Kindergarten*. Amen.

Chapter 36

Sleigh Me!

Since December began, I've been asked, "Are you finished with Christmas?" My answer is always yes, but I am not referring to my shopping list. I am done. Truly finished. Sad to say, but right now, I am simply tired of the whole season. The fat guy in the red suit had better look out. Don't even get me started on Rudolph. We all know his nose should be brown anyway.

Instead of being a perky, joyous mommy, I have become Santa's pimp. And he is my b—… well, you know. I have used him to break up fights, to get my children to brush their teeth, pick up their toys, and wash their hair. I use him and abuse him. "If you guys do not brush your teeth, Santa will not bring toys; he will only bring you mint dental floss, baking-soda toothpaste, and a toothbrush with firm bristles." You see, kids are more complicated these days, so I had to step it up a notch from the boring "bag of coal" routine. Besides, fossil fuels interest them.

My kids, a.k.a. Ike and Tina, seem to argue all of the time. Again, interject Santa into the picture. "Mommy, doesn't Santa say, 'Merry Christmas to all, and to all a good *fight*'?" I guess I'll be adding *Hooked on Phonics* to my shopping list. Well, they know if they continue to fight, all they will get under the tree is a Rock'em Sock'em Robots game *minus* the robots. Wanna box? Here it is, my little ones! Mental note: build up children's nest egg for future psychiatry visits.

I am trying to snap out of my grouchiness and get into the Christmas spirit. The Christmas play helped but only temporarily. I've been getting up early, before the kids awaken, to have coffee, plan my day, say my prayers, and just breathe. I also plug in the Christmas tree to add a bit of ambience to the moment. I must admit something to you about my tree. This year I have stepped into the realm of *artificial.* Yes, I know. But when you are a busy mom, a real tree becomes just another burden. I have to feed it, water it, trim it, and clean up after it. I do not need one more thing in the house to take care of.

To lighten things up, I'll share a little Christmas ditty that I wrote while decorating my lead-based tree from China. Here it goes:

Jingle bells, something smells
And it is not my tree,
This year we went artificial,
Prelit with a twenty-year warranty!

Now, no mold spores or sweeping chores
Just green plastic resin, and fume-y PVC
But no trimming needed or watering
or dangerous combustibility!

Oh! Jingle bells, please don't tell
For the children do not know
That Mommy paid the Fed-Ex fella
And opened the branches just like an umbrella*

Jingle bells, I have an old tree stand to sell
And I'll give you a very special deal
For our tradition has changed this year …
Fake is the new real!

*Rhythm problem acknowledged. So, if you are thinking of stealing my ditty, think otherwise, Mr. Plagiarizer. It is copyrighted, and, no, you blonds out there, that does not mean that you have the right to copy it. Ho! Ho! Ho!

Chapter 37

Claus for Alarm

Well, Christmas has passed, and I'm still trying to take a few toys out of their hermetically sealed packaging. When I was a child, I do not ever recall my parents using box cutters, skill saws, or expletives to open my toys. Just pull off a piece of tape, open the cardboard tab, and voila, your toy is ready to go. Not these days. My daughter's Ariel Barbie came wrapped in many layers of impenetrable plastic. Underneath the plastic, Barbie was held down against her will by a wire-tie straight jacket. I guess all the years of having to look perfect and maintain that one-inch waistline have caught up with old Barbie. She must be restrained. She did manage to keep smiling, though. What denial.

My son's toys were just as difficult to open and then required complex assembly only to be deciphered if you can read German, French, and Spanish. Oh, I see, turn the booklet over, now I can read it. All boy toys need at least ten megawatt batteries, have multiple parts, and make obnoxious sounds. My husband liked the machismo, destructive edge to the toys. He beamed with pride when my son started playing with them. Until he started carrying around Ariel Barbie day after day. Environmental or hereditary? I'll get back to you in about twenty years.

I should have expected what came next. Someone with three or four kids warned me it was going to happen. I started hearing voices. Strange, electronic cow noises, warped quacking, and "I am Furby" coming from various places in my home. At first, I thought my son was a ventriloquist, an advancement from the sign language, you know. Then, I realized that a hefty percentage of the Christmas toys make sounds, and they do it when the switch is *off*. See, the toys have trouble being idle, too. They remind you to play with them by talking, squeaking, or honking. "Hey, remember me, the fuzzy, orange tiger that tumbles?" "Please, please pick me up before your mother smashes me with a hammer." Great, more creatures in the house that need constant attention.

One doll, in particular, is especially needy. She recites, "I want to be your best friend. Hold me. Feed me. Am I pretty? Does my rear look fat in these pants?" Sorry, that last one automatically plays in my head. Anyway, Anita Frynd, as I call her, became mildly possessed when her battery supply was low. In a voice that would make Linda Blair proud, she started giving hypnotic commands—with the power *off*. Too freaky. I had to perform an exorcism and promptly remove all four triple As.

I'll certainly be prepared next year for the barrage of Santa questions. My precocious little girl wanted to know if the reindeer will mess up the blue Katrina tarps when they land on the rooftops. I told her the tarps allow the sleigh to have a smoother landing.

"What if Santa has to potty?" she asked curiously.

I made up a good one, I think. I said that the sleigh is equipped with a concealed, state-of-the-art port-o-let with tinsel toilet paper to boot.

"Are Santa and Jesus best friends, Mommy?"

"Honey, this is why I send you to Catholic school." Merry Christmas.

Chapter 38

Tsumommy!

As I sit here to write, I am thankful that I am upright, breathing air through my nostrils, and that my joints feel normal. You see, I have been in bed with the flu for five days. The real flu. Influenza type A. If you know me, type A would be the strain that I would get. Any other five days out of the year would have been acceptable, but not December 22 through December 27. Moms just cannot be sick, especially at Christmas. When Mother is sick, the Earth shifts slightly off its axis, sending waves of disarray into the household. I'll call it a Tsumommy—with mass destruction followed by a cleanup and then recovery. I can also compare it to having the main server of a computer network going down, a car engine throwing a rod during a trip across country, or, better yet, the cable going out.

I have heard repeatedly from others that "it is going around." That particular statement is a pet peeve of mine, and come to think of it, the word *peeve* itself is annoying. I mean, have you ever heard *peeve* used in any other context? Another word that bothers me is *uncanny*, as in "She looks so much like Diane Sawyer, it's uncanny!" So what about canny? Do we ever hear that word in a sentence? Can you tell I've had a lot of time on my hands through this illness? My brain is not designed to be idle according to the latest professional I have visited. Seriously, aren't things always "going around"? If not, whom do they start and end with? Me, I guess.

So it goes, a memorable Christmas with Mommy entertaining the kids with the fever and chills show. No kidding. Santa and his cruel elves made a puppet theater for my daughter, and it came with five puppets including a ballerina, a chef, a surgeon, a horse, and a cheerleader. A creative, interactive toy that requires the full attention of an adult. Just what I needed with a fever of 102 and a body that could not go vertical. The puppets and their big sewn-on eyes beckoned to be played with. They kept looking at me, and I could read the look on their fuzzy faces. I even think they started talking to me as I lay in a heap on the sofa. Are hallucinations a symptom of the flu? Well, the ballerina puppet said to me, "Take tutu aspirins, and call me in the morning." The puppet chef, in a French accent, said, "Brie, your face is beet red, and you need to be whisked away to the hospital immediately, chop, chop." The surgeon puppet offered a breast lift and a Botox injection. *Offer noted.* The horse said, "Hay, I took a gallop poll, and the flu is going around. It would behoove you to go to the doctor before your lungs get trifected. Oh, and by the way, I am a gift horse, so don't look me in the mouth." The cheerleader puppet was next. She had the nerve to tell me, "Two bits." Oh, wait, sorry, I think the horse said that too. She shouted to me through her megaphone, "Cheers," and then took a shot from a flask hidden in her pompoms. Cheerleading is a sport, you know, and she was very d-e-f-e-n-s-i-v-e about it. It is never recognized as such, so this must be why she turned to the bottle. Turns out to have been Evian spring water. Too many calories in liquor, I guess.

Santa is not on my nice list. He brought very loud and brain-penetrating noisemakers to my son. A truck with a screeching back-up sound, a train that sounds like a tornado coming, and a fire engine with emergency lights and an ambulance siren. My aching head could barely take it, but I had to put on a smile when he brought them to me, over and over, with his excited little face saying, "Look, Mommy!" I was secretly planning a covert mission to destroy all batteries in the house. Seriously, my mind locked in on the flashing lights of the toys, and it was like the Terminator took over me. Unfortunately, I could not coordinate my throbbing wrist joints to turn the little screw that opens the battery pack.

Well, I've officially exited the woods, and I'm feeling much better. The children have their mommy back, even though it is at half speed. My husband can now go back full force to his job and can hang up his Mr. Mom hat for now. I give him credit for being an excellent nurse and housekeeper while I was sick. I got the message from above, loud and clear, to slow down a bit. This will be my New Year's resolution (along with being first in line to get a flu shot).

Chapter 39

Throw Me Something, Mister

This morning I woke up with a spring in my step and a song in my head. The spring in my step was actually a Slinky that my son left on the floor next to my slippers. And the song playing in my head was Simon and Garfunkel's "The Sounds of Silence." My house is quiet, and it is a welcomed sound, indeed. The kids are back in school, and I can finally take a breather. On Monday morning, when I came home to an empty house, I joyously twirled like I was Julie Andrews in *The Sound of Music.* I could say that I've been feeling von Trapped at home with my children over the holidays. I think we were all experiencing an acute case of cabin fever. Although each of my children had mounds of Christmas presents to play with, I still heard, "We are bored." I told them to play their board games, but my daughter didn't think that was very funny.

Now, I have a little extra time on my hands to get my to-do list in order without interruption. First on the list is to organize my linen closet and a few kitchen drawers that aren't sorted, aligned, and labeled yet. This isn't a New Year's resolution, it is simply part of my little "problem," appropriately labeled, "obsessive-compulsive disorder." (Note more labeling.) I have been officially diagnosed by Dr. Google.com (along with lactose intolerance and premenopausal symptoms).

I consider myself organized, and normally I do not have any problem disposing of things that aren't useful to me. Frequent trips to Goodwill enable me to keep the kids' toys and general clutter to a minimum. While they are at school, I invade their closets like a cat burglar and place toys they never play with into my Goodwill bag. I usually dress in black but not for discreetness—for slimness, of course. In the interim, I hide the bag deep in my trunk and cover it with a jumper cable kit and a portable air compressor. Occasionally, they will discover a pointed corner of an old toy piercing through the bag or a tuft of hair from a baby doll. Then, I have lots of 'splaining to do.

However, there are a few things I just can't throw away. And they all seem to talk to me right before I shove them in a large plastic garbage bag. I'll share my list of "talking" items to see if you hear them, too.

1. *Old towels.* I have a wonderful collection of shredded, bleached-out towels that I cannot throw or give away. My towels look like surrender flags from the War of 1812. I get a warm, fuzzy feeling (but not from my towels) when I look through bed and bath catalogs that show fluffy, perfectly folded, matching towels neatly arranged in a linen closet. I desperately want that closet, but my towels whisper, "Please don't throw me out. I've dried you off since high school. I'm like family. What if the washing-machine hose becomes disconnected and the house starts to flood? You will need me and all the others, too!" Good point. I'll keep them another year.
2. *Tote bags, duffel bags, and small luggage.* The difficulty experienced here must be a remnant from my prehistoric nomad days. My genetic makeup tells me to always be prepared for a disaster. Whether it is a drought, a coming Ice Age, or even a locust invasion, I've got bags! Bear in mind that women are *gatherers.* My latest count: eleven tote bags, three duffel bags, and six small suitcases. When I climb into the attic to organize my travel items, I start hearing voices again. The tote bag reminds me that one day I can use it to carry groceries home from the hip, organic-food store. I will buy some alfalfa sprouts, tofu hot dogs, wheat grass, and quinoa and forego the plastic bags. For now, plastic bags prevail and so do Ball Park franks. The duffel bags don't talk, but if they did, I imagine they would have a goofy, deep voice and not be too intelligent (like Elaine's boyfriend, Puddy, from *Seinfeld*). The most loquacious of the bunch is the carry-on luggage. When I try to give away one in particular, it tells me, "Picture us at the airport, getting ready for a flight to the Caribbean. I am so convenient, and I have wheels, too. I can fit everything you need right here. I know I am stained and have large, purple poppies all over me, but look what Hollywood is wearing these days. Besides, I was a graduation gift from your great aunt (who is dead, *remember*!).

You wouldn't dishonor her by giving me away, now would you?" OK, I'll keep you, too.

3. *Holey underwear.* And I'm not talking about the Pope's boxer shorts. I admit to possessing a few pairs of exceptionally comfortable but very anti–Victoria's Secret undergarments that are worn only in the house. Mom always said, "Wear nice underwear in case you are ever in a car accident." Only women can worry about such things. Besides, it is not like emergency personnel would refuse treatment on me because of ratty underwear. But I have imagined the police officer at the scene writing up the accident report and giggling when he notes, "Fifty feet of skid marks."
4. *Plastic parade cups.* The best in fine dining. Who wouldn't want a nice refreshing drink out of a plastic cup advertising "Sam's Sewer Tank Cleaning"? One year, I rode on a Mardi Gras float, and I was astounded by how excited people got over a plastic cup. It was like I was throwing pure gold bullions to the masses. When the cup hit the ground in the crowd, the ensuing fight outshined the Ultimate Fighting championship match. Ironically, the cup I was throwing had an advertisement for "Glenda's Glassware and Home Store." Anyway, my assortment of cups speaks to me as well. They tell me, "What if forty people unexpectedly show up at your door, and they are all incredibly thirsty? Remember the drought? You will need extra cups! All forty-three of us can save the moment with three to spare! Plus, look how easily we are stacked. You know how you like orderly stacks. We simply do not take up enough space to justify tossing us out." Enough said, I'll keep you.
5. *Old makeup or costume jewelry.* When it is time to sort through these items, I always visualize myself getting dressed for an elaborate costume ball. What if I need those disco platform shoes one day? And it would be a tragedy if I discarded the mullet wig, only to need it for the ball!

So, before 2009 rolls around, I am committed to pack away my old towels, plastic cups, tote bags, underwear, and the red and white fringed cowgirl shirt. Oh, and I plan on delivering them to Goodwill in a bright purple poppy suitcase.

Chapter 40

Going Digital

With the month of January almost over, I am sure everyone has been faithfully sticking to their New Year's resolutions. Pounds have been lost, cigarettes have been thrown away for good, and steamed veggies have replaced French fries. My three-year-old is adjusting well to the changes, but he has been incessantly humming the little ditty, "Winston takes good …" I joke, but it is true that my household has been trying to break a few bad habits.

For one, my daughter, who started sucking her thumb in utero, has now become conscious of her habit. Everywhere we go, someone always manages to ask her, "Is that thumb good?" She used to answer, "Why, yes, it is! You should try it. It is very comforting and is conveniently located on my distal upper limb, and my mommy does not have to spend money on pacifiers." But now she avoids the question better than a seasoned politician. She responds, "Well, it depends on what you mean by *good*."

So, now she has started to really think about stopping. Poor darling came up to me the other day and excitedly said, "Mommy, I know how I can stop sucking my thumb! I can get one of those patches I saw on television! It helps people who smoke, and maybe they make one for the thumb!" A good name for it would be Digitalis.

We have promised her a puppy if she stops sucking her thumb by her seventh birthday. This is only four months away, and there doesn't seem to be any inkling of sucking cessation. I am secretly wishing she does not stop because I *do not* want a puppy in the house. I feel like I have a litter right now. Whining at night, lots of attention, chewing up furniture, and messing on the floor. Yep, I am there already. One more mouth to feed will put me over the top. I wonder if puppies eat Fruit Loops.

With my brain being in a fog most of the time, I am concerned that I may deworm my kids and give a Flintstone vitamin to the puppy. I might even whistle for the kids to come, sit, and stay. This might not be a bad idea, but I certainly won't ask them to shake or roll over in front of anyone.

I may not sound like an active member of PETA, but I really do love dogs. Our Labrador retriever, Sam, is a wonderful pet, and he may even like the addition of a puppy to our family. At least he would have someone to play with. Before our kids were born, Sam was the center of attention. We would play Frisbee, and he would accompany me on my daily runs. He was clean and shiny and was only given premium dog food. On my desk at work was his picture, which was framed in a contemporary bone pattern with randomly placed puppy prints. It was really a piece of art, let me tell you. Now he is lucky to get the Ol' Roy dog food brand from Wal-Mart and play an occasional game of fetch. The game goes like this: the ball is thrown once, he retrieves, game over. Then I cross off "play with dog" from my to-do list.

I have accidentally called the dog my son's name and vice versa. It is usually when he is about to pee on something he isn't supposed to—the dog that is. My son sneaks dog food to eat, too. I've caught him in the corner munching down on Alpo thinking it was the best thing in the world. If you ever tasted my cooking, maybe you would agree. I don't think it has affected him very much, but I have noticed that he nervously scratches at the back door during a lightning storm, and he snaps in midair at horseflies. Typical three-year-old behavior, I guess.

Aside from the Thumbelina situation, we are trying to improve in other areas. Recycling is a good example. In the past, I've tried to recycle diapers, but it didn't work out too well. Maybe I should have switched to cloth diapers. As a matter of fact, the recycling center has blacklisted me.

Television is another issue. I have significantly cut back the time the kids can watch TV—it is my duty as a mother. I only allow it from 7:00 a.m. to 5:00 p.m. It seems to be working for everyone. It has improved their math skills and number recognition. Both kids can recite the phone number of the personal injury attorney who has bought every thirty-second spot available on television. When my little girl fell off of her bike the other day, she was ready to contact him. If the thumb patch causes any skin irritation or flare-ups of eczema and is recalled by the FDA, we know who to call.

Chapter 41

Seamus on You

This week, as I was driving around town looking at all the shamrock decorations, leprechauns, and advertisements for green beer parties, it dawned on me that St. Patrick's Day is really a man's holiday. Valentine's Day is clearly for women, so it is only fair for the guys to have a turn. March 17 turns out to be just perfect for the male species. For one, there isn't a present or a card involved, they do not have to match their clothes, and women will kiss them for a paper flower regardless of how drunk and un-Irish they are. Yes, Salvador and Dominick will get as much affection as Liam and Seamus at the Irish parade.

On the subject of men, I started thinking about how uncomplicated their lives are when it comes to things such as haircuts, clothing, and their basic personal-hygiene routine. This revelation came to me when I was at the barbershop with my little boy. The barbershop is a cultural experience for women. When I'm there, I kind of feel like the lone husband you see at Victoria's Secret, completely out of his element but still enjoying the scenery. One could call it Venus envy.

The barbershop has a handwritten sign that says, "Haircuts 10 dollars." Simple, to the point, no questions asked. At a women's salon, ten dollars will get you a haircut, but it is literally a hair cut, just one hair. There aren't any gumball machines, sports paraphernalia, or antlers at a salon. Actually, I take back the antler comment after my recent foil-highlight experience. Another thing that intrigues me about the barbershop is that men do not give the barber much instruction on how they want their hair cut. They just get in the chair and put faith in the barber to buzz them the right way. They do not worry about face shape, bangs, or layers. Before my haircut, I buy several haircutting magazines and use about four hundred sticky notes to mark my favorite cuts. I bring this in to my hairdresser, and we have a "sit-down." I tell her, "I like this one, but I want it a little shorter but with more layers, but not too short because of my round face. Oh, and look at this one, do you think you could cut the back like this but leave the front like the last one? Remember, I'm not very good at styling it, so I need a manageable cut, and I still want to be able to put it in a ponytail." By the time I've finished going over the blueprints for my new haircut, the stylist is ready to give me a good head shaving.

When it comes to clothing and fashion, men are fuss-free once again. For example, men do not care if they wear black pants and navy shirts. This ensemble obviously opposes the laws of nature, but does it bother them? No, not one bit. Does it bother me? To the core, I must say. In regards to a personal-hygiene routine, the XY chromosomes prevail again. First of all, the shear square footage of skin to be shaved is much less than a woman. We are talking cheeks, chin, and upper lip here. Big deal. For women, we have to shave both legs, the tops of our toes (yes, men, there is hair there, just look down), the upper lip for some of our hirsute sisters, delicate armpits with many angles, and bikini lines, too. When was the last time a man took a sharp instrument near there? Well, boys, we do it all the time, so quit griping unless you've had a vasectomy. Then comes the body lotion and exfoliation. We use one type for the face, one for just the eyes, then the body, and also the heels. My husband does not even use lotion, and his skin is well hydrated. It is simply not fair. He thinks exfoliation has something to do with Reynolds aluminum wrap.

Each Sunday, I think about what lessons I've learned from my experiences of the week. At the barbershop, my son had to wait his turn, and I could not interject my thoughts on the intricacies of little-boy haircuts. So this week, my lessons came from the barbershop. I learned to practice patience, remember the art of listening, and simply have faith. What a great lesson.

Chapter 42

Just My Luck

The summerlike weather we have been experiencing this past week has brought warmth to my days in ways other than just a temperature increase. My soul feels light and excited as I recall my childhood days, when I spent most of the daylight hours outdoors, exploring the world before me and creating meaningful inventory for me to call upon as a busy adult.

My daughter recently opened an old book of mine and found a cluster of four-leaf clovers, pressed ever so neatly between the pages. Granted, they were a bit crumbly but still intact and fascinating for her to see. I explained how difficult they were to find and out of a patch of one thousand regular clovers, there may be only a few four-leaf clovers or none at all.

"Wow!" she said. "They must be very special, Mommy. Is this why you saved them in a book?"

"Yes, honey, they are a symbol of luck," I told her.

Well, this started the quest for locating fresh four-leaf clovers of her own.

So every evening we have ventured out to our neighbor's field to look for four-leaf clovers. The kids love this. They study the honeybees on the clover flowers and wonder about the pollen pockets on their legs. My little boy thought the bees had "big yellow muscles" on their legs, but my daughter corrected him swiftly, having learned about insects at school.

After a few days of clover hunting, we came back empty handed but happy. There is something about looking for four-leaf clovers that is quite relaxing and Zen. On the day before the grass was to be cut, we had one last look and scoured the field. Well, we hit a payload. My husband found a hybrid patch of clover that yielded a total of four lucky ones! Yes! My daughter immediately decided that each four-leaf clover represented a member of our family. We went home and placed the clovers in her favorite book. I'm hoping she will forget they are there so that in about ten years, she can open the book with surprise and fondly remember seeking them, picking them, and the warm feeling of family.

The clover experience led to other excursions that I have planned for my children. A nostalgic checklist for us to experience this summer. I am tired of the Disney Channel keeping their attention and influencing them. They need a healthy dose of nature. I decided to get an early start by taking them to find blackberries on my dad's farm. I showed them how they grow on sticker bushes and how to carefully pick them. They were amazed that we could eat them on the spot and that Mommy did not wash the berries or even their grubby little hands. We all had seeded smiles, purple tongues, and stained fingernails, but it was great! After we picked berries, I took them over to a low-slung branch on a live-oak tree where a rope swing hangs. I did examine the rope for ants and other creepy crawlers, but I didn't worry about any safety issues that I normally obsess over. For example, I like to check the tensile strength of the swings at parks and spray down the seats with Lysol before strapping them in and buckling on their helmets. This time I let them go. I pushed them high and prayed that their petite fingers could hold on for the duration. Pure bliss would best describe the look on their faces.

Next on our list is locating a pond with tadpoles squirming around. I often refer to my kids as tadpoles, among other endearing terms such as honey bears, sweetie pies, piglets, snuggle bunnies, little chimps, and jumping beans. I won't go into any pet names that I call my husband. He would be too embarrassed. Well, all right, I'll share a few. "Honey" (which is followed by "will you take out the garbage?"), "Sweetie" (followed by "the grass needs cutting before it rains"), and "Babe" (followed by "do you need anything from Target?"). Really exciting, I know.

Well, our list goes on to include sucking nectar from honeysuckles, chasing fireflies, making homemade ice cream, and planting watermelon seeds. Then there is the old avocado seed sprouting on the kitchen windowsill idea. Does anyone ever grow an avocado from that? I've never seen one, but, growing up, we always had one by the sink. Maybe it is a symbol of luck, too.

Clearly, life's message is from the clover patch. To me, everyday experiences are like the three-leaf clovers. Necessary, predictable, and abundant. The four-leaf clovers represent extraordinary times. Rare, magical, but ever present if you just expect them. Expect them.

Author's Biography

Brenna Barzenick is a married mother of two children. She is a licensed physical therapist and a 1994 graduate of Louisiana State University Medical Center, School of Allied Health Professions in New Orleans, Louisiana. Brenna was the owner of a successful private practice before selling it to become a full-time mom—a job that has inspired her to write.

Brenna is the author of a popular newspaper column in the *Daily Star* called "Tales from the Crib." She resides in her hometown of Hammond, Louisiana, with her family.

Printed in the United States
137191LV00004B/6/P

9 780595 491346